CROCHET YOUR OWN DOG

Crochet Your Own Dog
Published in 2024 by Zakka Workshop,
a division of World Book Media LLC

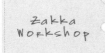

www.zakkaworkshop.com
134 Federal Street
Salem, MA 01970
info@zakkaworkshop.com

DAKKOSHITAKUNARU AMIGURUMI WANKO
Copyright ©2020 Mieko Shindo
All rights reserved.

Original Japanese edition published by NIHONBUNGEISHA Co., Ltd. English translation rights arranged with NIHONBUNGEISHA Co., Ltd. through Japan UNI Agency, Inc., Tokyo. English language rights, translation & production by World Book Media, LLC.

Publisher: Yoshichika Yoshida
Editor: Takashi Makino
Editor: Mie Takechi
Design: Chiyomi Ito
Photography: Shimane Michimasa
Diagrams and Technical Illustrations: Midorinokuma
Translation: Kyoko Matthews
English Editor: Lindsay Fair
Technical Editor: Lynne Rowe

ISBN: 978-1-940552-83-5

Printed in China

10 9 8 7 6 5 4 3 2 1

CROCHET YOUR OWN DOG

14 LIFE-SIZE AMIGURUMI PUPS TO MAKE AND LOVE!

Mieko Shindo

Contents

Introduction

It all starts with a simple ball of yarn and a crochet hook. Stitch by stitch, the face and body begin to take shape. Then, as soon as the eyes and nose are attached, a cute little dog comes to life as if by magic.

Crocheted dogs have the power to bring a smile to people's faces, whether you're the one making them or you're the one receiving them as a gift. And if the crocheted dog resembles a real canine in your life, the feeling is even more special. In fact, my very own dog served as the model for the toy poodle design!

This book includes 14 patterns representing 10 different dog breeds. First, you'll crochet a head, body, legs, and a tail, and then stuff and assemble the different parts. Next, you'll learn how to create realistic looking fur using a unique yarn grafting method. You'll even use real dog grooming brushes to capture the authentic look and feel of a dog's coat.

You can customize the yarn colors to match your own furry friend and have fun trimming and styling the fur until you achieve the desired look. I hope that you enjoy the process of creating your very own crocheted dogs and that they bring as much happiness to your life as they have to mine!

—Mieko Shindo

Toy Poodle / Sit

This adorable puppy sports a
curly coat with longer hair at
the ears. Use a slicker brush
made for dog grooming to
loosen the yarn and create
curls that are characteristic of
a toy poodle's coat.

Instructions 🐾 **Page 61**

Teddy bear cuts are a popular choice for poodles as this grooming style complements thick coats. Use bulky yarn to achieve this fluffy look.

Instructions 🐾 🐾 **Page 66**

Papillon / Sit

Papillons are known for their large, wing-shaped ears. In fact, "papillon" means butterfly in French! To achieve their distinguished look, a lot of decorative fur is added to the ears and chest, creating an elegant appearance.

Instructions 🐾 🐾 **Page 71**

Long Haired Chihuahua / Lie Down

Chihuahuas may be small, but they are full of energy! This cream and white colored Chihuahua features large eyes and a small body, which makes for a cute combination.

Instructions 🐾 **Page 76**

Black and tan is also a popular color combination for Chihuahuas. The contrast between the dark and light fur makes this dog appear as if it has eyebrows! This breed is so small in real life that this version made from yarn is nearly true to size.

Instructions 🐾 🐾 Page 81

Pomeranian / Sit

Pomeranians often have long, voluminous, brightly colored fur referred to as red or orange. Their cute smiling faces have a fox-like resemblance that's hard to resist.

Instructions   **Page 86**

𝒫omeranian / Stand

Pomeranians are known for being vivacious and active dogs. This black and tan Pomeranian features lighter fur markings above the eyes, at the muzzle, and on the chest.

Instructions  **Page 91**

Dachshund / Lie Down

This cream colored dachshund has such a sweet look! Use a wool felting needle on the fur around the face, following the contours of the head.

Instructions 🐾 🐾 **Page 96**

Dachshund / Stand

Combine four different colors of yarn to create this more complex fur featuring subtle shading. Dachshunds exhibit lots of brown color variations, so experiment with different combinations.

Instructions 🐾 🐾 **Page 100**

Maltese / Sit

Maltese dogs have been popular pets dating as far back as ancient Egypt and Greece. Use pure white yarn to capture the soft, snowy look of the Maltese's coat.

Instructions 🐾 🐾 **Page 104**

Miniature Schnauzer / Sit

Schnauzers are known for their salt and pepper colored fur.
To create this stylish, well-groomed look, leave the yarn for
the paws a bit longer and trim it into a boot shape.

Instructions 🐾 🐾 **Page 109**

Long haired Chihuahua in cream and white

Long haired Chihuahua in black and white

Shih Tzu

Is it dinnertime yet?

35

Shih Tzu / Lie Down

Shih Tzus are known for being impeccably groomed. Mix different shades of brown to create the mottled markings around the eyes and ears, and graft yarn around the nose to create the cute, distinctively round-shaped face.

Instructions 🐾 🐾 **Page 114**

Yorkshire Terrier / Sit

Yorkies are known for their silky coats of steel blue and golden tan. This breed's long hair provides an opportunity to try fun hairstyles and add accessories, such as the ribbon shown here.

Instructions 🐾 ✂ **Page 118**

Bichon Frise / Stand

These dogs are known for their fluffy white fur that resembles a cotton ball, especially when groomed into a rounded shape.

Instructions 🐾 🐾 Page 123

Tools & Materials

(1) Needle felting claw

Use to loosen and arrange the yarn, especially when working detailed areas such as around the eyes. This tool is made by Clover.

(2) Grooming scissors

Use to trim yarn into shape after grafting. Designed specifically for grooming, these scissors can be purchased online or at a pet supply store.

(3) Yarn scissors

Use to cut pieces of yarn to length.

(4) Slicker brush

This tool is normally used for grooming real dogs. In this book, it is used to loosen grafted yarn.

(5) Yarn threader

Use to thread tapestry needles with yarn.

(6) Stitch markers

Attach into crochet stitches for counting rows and rounds.

(7) Sewing pins

Use to fix body parts in position.

(8) Tapestry needle

Use a needle with a large eye designed for yarn or thick thread to attach body parts and graft yarn.

(9) Felting needle

This type of needle is sold as a refill to be used with a needle felting pen. In this book, the needle is used on its own when grafting yarn.

(10) Crochet hooks

Use to crochet the body parts for the dogs.

(11) Craft glue

Use to glue toy safety noses and eyes in place. Look for a bottle with a thin nozzle for easy application.

(12) Animal toy safety noses

These black plastic noses are available in a variety of different sizes, including 18 mm, 20 mm, 21 mm, and 23 mm. They come with a washer that is used to secure the nose in place on the inside of the stuffed animal, but can also be glued on if the dog isn't intended as a child's toy (see health and safety note below).

(13) Animal toy safety eyes

These black plastic eye buttons are available in a variety of sizes, including 15 mm and 18 mm. Just like the noses, they come with washers that are used to secure the eyes in place on the inside of the stuffed animal, but can also be glued on if the dog isn't intended as a child's toy (see health and safety note below).

> **Health and Safety Note:** Toy safety eyes and noses are not suitable for children under the age of three as they pose a choking hazard. For safety reasons, if your dog is intended to be used a child's toy, use a tapestry needle and black or brown yarn to embroider the eyes and a nose instead. If you are using toy safety eyes and noses, make sure you follow the manufacturer's instructions.

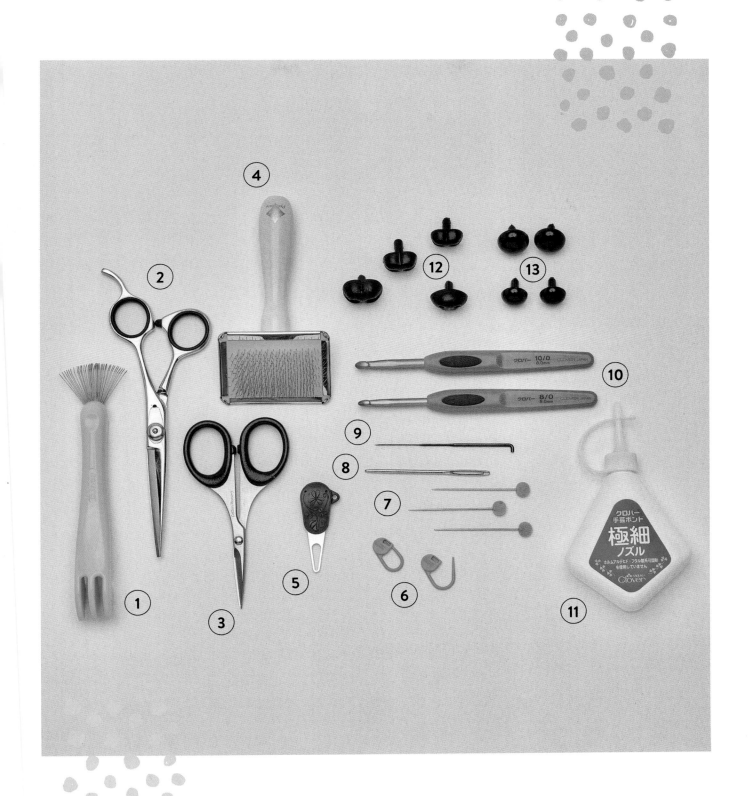

How to Crochet Your Own Dog

The following instructions outline the basic construction steps for all of the dogs in this book. This includes instructions for assembling the dogs into three different poses: sit, stand, and lie down. Refer to pages 45–60 for more detailed tutorials on crocheting and assembling the dogs and pages 61–127 for project instructions for each type of dog.

Basic Construction Steps

Most of the dogs in this book are composed of 10 crocheted body parts (a few have a different style ear that is not crocheted, so they are only composed of 8). Once assembled, these body parts will become the foundation for grafting yarn to create the fur.

1. Crochet each body part. Instructions are provided in both written and chart form. Always leave a 12" (30 cm) thread tail when you finish crocheting a body part, unless otherwise noted. These will be used to sew the body parts together when assembling the stuffed animal.

2. Fill each body part with polyester stuffing, except for the ears. Aim for the same firmness as when stuffing a pillow.

3. Sew the body parts together following the instructions for the desired pose (refer to page 55). Attach the toy safety nose and eyes, following the manufacturer's instructions, or embroider the eyes and nose with yarn if the dog is intended as a child's toy (see health and safety note on page 42).

4. Graft the yarn to create the fur.

5. Loosen the yarn with a slicker brush and trim it into shape.

6. Continue brushing and trimming the fur as desired. Use a felting needle to compress the yarn in the specific areas noted, such as around the eyes and ears.

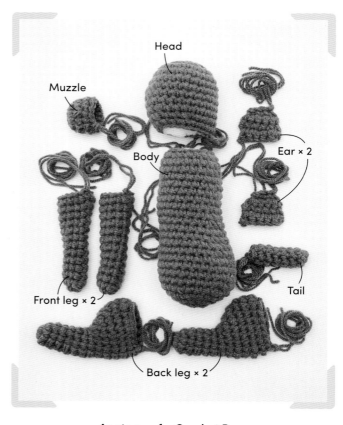

Anatomy of a Crochet Dog

US vs UK Crochet Terminology

US and UK crochet terms have different meanings, so it's important to check which style was used to write the pattern. Please note that this book uses US crochet terms. The chart below highlights the differences in terminology.

US	UK
single crochet (sc)	double crochet (dc)
half double crochet cluster (hdc-cl)	half treble crochet cluster (htc-cl)

Abbreviations	
beg	beginning
ch	chain
g	grams
rnd	round
sc	single crochet
slst	slip stitch
st(s)	stitch(es)
tog	together
yd(s)	yard(s)

Make a Magic Ring

This starting technique is used for all the body parts, except the muzzles and ears for some of the dogs. The following photos show the yarn held double, but refer to the project instructions for the number of strands to use for each type of dog.

01 Set the hook behind the yarn and bring the hook toward the front in a counterclockwise direction.

02 The yarn is wrapped around the hook, making a loop.

03 The yarn that was under the thumb in step 2 is crossed as shown in the photo above.

04 Yarn over the hook and pull through the loop.

05 Yarn is now on the hook, ready to begin.

Crochet the Body

x = Single crochet

01 Yarn over the hook and pull through again (chain stitch).

02 The first chain of the round is complete.

03 Insert the hook into the center of the loop again.

04 Yarn over and pull loop through.

05 There are two loops on the hook.

06 Yarn over and pull through two loops.

07 The first single crochet is complete. This is noted with an x symbol in the crochet charts.

08 Attach a stitch marker into the first single crochet stitch of the first round. This will serve as a guide so that you will know where the second round starts.

09 Repeat steps 3–7 five more times to make 6 single crochet stitches in total.

10 The first 6 single crochet stitches are complete.

11 Remove the hook temporarily and pull on the starting tail end of yarn to close the magic ring. Make sure you hold on to the stitches and don't let them unravel.

12 The magic ring is now closed and the stitches are now a circle shape.

13 Insert the hook back into the working loop. Close the round by inserting the hook into either the first single crochet (under top loops of stitch), or under the beginning chain 1 (if directed in your pattern).

14 Yarn over and pull loop through all loops (slip stitch) to close the round. Remove marker.

01 Make one chain stitch (beginning stitch for second round).

02 Insert the hook into the first single crochet of the previous round (the one that held the marker) and make one single crochet.

03 Replace your stitch marker in the top of the stitch just made.

04 Insert the hook at the same position as the first stitch and make another single crochet (make two single crochets into the same stitch).

05 Make two single crochets into each of the remaining stitches from the first round. You now have 12 single crochet stitches. Refer to individual project instructions to crochet the additional rounds.

Crochet the Muzzle

01 Make five chain stitches.

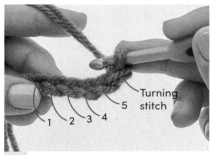

02 Make one chain stitch as a turning stitch.

03 Insert the hook at the 5th chain stitch through one side.

04 Make one single crochet.

05 Attach a stitch marker in the first stitch as a guide where to start the second round.

06 Make a single crochet in the next stitch.

07 Make more single crochet stitches (to reach the end of the chain).

08 Make one more single crochet in the end stitch.

09 There are now two single crochet stitches in the end stitch.

10 Rotate the piece and make another single crochet in the end stitch.

11 There are now three single crochet stitches in the end stitch.

12 Working along the opposite side of the chain stitches, work four single crochet stitches to reach the end.

13 Make another single crochet in the end stitch.

14 Join the round with a slip stitch, either into the first single crochet or into the beginning chain 1 (as noted in the individual project instructions).

15 The first round of the muzzle is complete. Refer to individual project instructions to crochet the additional rounds.

Crochet the Back Legs

01 Starting with a magic ring, work seven rounds of seven single crochet stitches.

02 For the 8th round, work three single crochet stitches.

03 In next stitch, work five single crochet stitches (all into the same stitch).

04 Work another three single crochet stitches to complete the round. This will be where the back leg folds.

Crochet the Paws

⚲ = Cluster stitch variation with 3 half double crochet

The papillon (page 71), long haired Chihuahuas (pages 76 and 81), and Yorkshire terrier (page 118) use the following technique to create the paws. The cluster stitch variation with three half double crochets creates little bumps that look like toes.

01 Starting with a magic ring, work eight single crochet stitches.

02 For the second round, make two single crochets (attaching a stitch marker in the first stitch to mark start of round).

03 Yarn over and insert hook in next stitch.

04 Yarn over and pull through, leaving the loop longer.

05 Repeat steps 3 and 4 in the same stitch; seven loops remain on the hook.

06 Yarn over and pull through six loops; two loops remain on the hook.

07 Yarn over and pull through the last two loops.

08 The cluster stitch variation with 3 half double crochet is completed.

09 Repeat the cluster stitch in next two stitches, then work two single crochets to complete the round.

Assemble the Body Parts

Stuff the individual body parts and sew together in the following order:

1. Attach the muzzle to the head

2. Attach the head, legs (see detailed instructions below), and tail to the body

3. Attach the ears to the head.

Use the yarn tails left at the end of crocheting each body part to sew everything together.

HOW TO ATTACH THE LEGS FOR THE SIT POSE

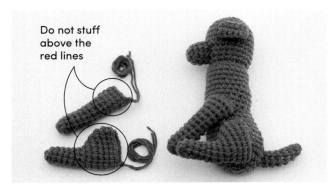

Do not stuff above the red lines

How to Stuff: Add stuffing to the feet, but not the parts of the legs that will be attached to the body. The areas outlined in red thread above serve as a guide for where the legs will attach to the body. Firmly stuff the other body parts (head, body, muzzle, and tail) for all poses.

01 Pin the back leg in place in the position noted on page 55.

02 Thread a tapestry needle with the 12" (30 cm) long yarn tail from the leg. Insert the needle under one stitch from the body.

03 Insert the needle behind the single crochet (vertical yarn) on the outside of the back leg.

 Note: You will be attaching the right side of the leg only.

04 Attach the body and the leg using mattress stitch (often called ladder stitch).

05 View of the leg and body as the mattress stitch is progressing.

06 The open area of the back leg is now attached.

07 Continue using mattress stitch to attach the inside of the leg to the body.

08 Sewing along the inside prevents the back leg from opening up and achieves that classic sitting pose.

09 Follow the same process to attach the front leg. Sew the first three rounds to the body along the inside of the leg.

HOW TO ATTACH THE LEGS FOR THE STAND POSE

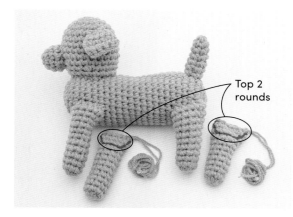

Top 2 rounds

How to Stuff: Add less stuffing at the top two rounds of the legs.

How to Attach the Legs to the Body: Fold the top of each leg under and sew to the body, following the red line as a guide.

HOW TO ATTACH THE LEGS FOR THE LIE DOWN POSE

Follow the same instruction for attaching the back legs for the sit pose on pages 53–54.

The Basic Poses

Once the body parts are complete, the dogs can be assembled in three different poses: sit, stand, and lie down. The guides below illustrate general body part placement for each pose. Refer to the individual project instructions for ear and muzzle placement for each type of dog.

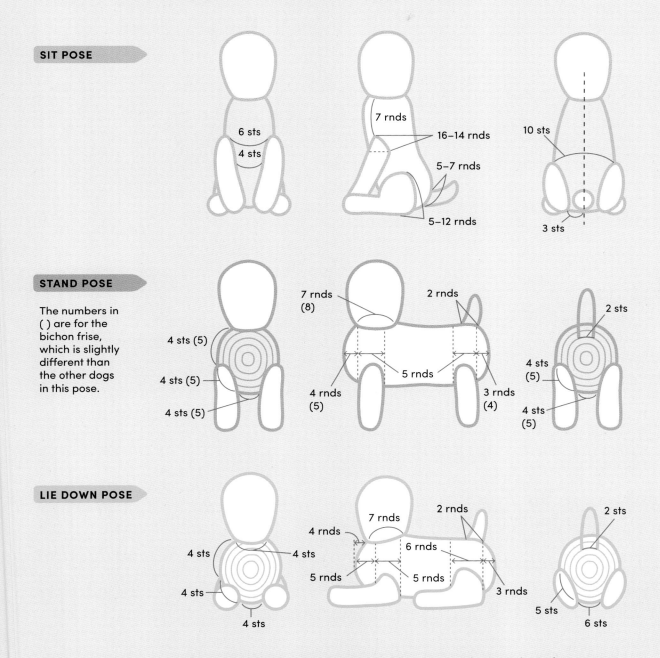

SIT POSE

6 sts
4 sts

7 rnds
16–14 rnds
5–7 rnds
5–12 rnds

10 sts
3 sts

STAND POSE

The numbers in ( ) are for the bichon frise, which is slightly different than the other dogs in this pose.

4 sts (5)
4 sts (5)
4 sts (5)

7 rnds (8)
2 rnds
5 rnds
4 rnds (5)
3 rnds (4)

2 sts
4 sts (5)
4 sts (5)

LIE DOWN POSE

4 sts
4 sts
4 sts
4 sts

4 rnds
7 rnds
2 rnds
6 rnds
5 rnds
5 rnds
3 rnds

2 sts
5 sts
6 sts

 Note: The size of your work may differ slightly from the examples in the book based on gauge. If your gauge is different than the examples in the book, you may need to adjust body part placement to achieve overall balance.

Graft the Fur

Grafting is the technique of attaching long strands of yarn to the crocheted body in order to create the look of fur. As a general rule, you'll use the same color yarn for grafting as used to crochet the foundation. Occasionally, additional colors of yarn are added to create subtle shading.

PREPARE THE YARN

Double 4 strands of yarn to create 8 strands

 Note: Use a yarn threader if you're having trouble threading the yarn onto the needle.

Align four strands of yarn. Thread onto a tapestry needle and fold in half so the yarn is doubled. There will now be eight strands. Trim the yarn to 24" (60 cm). For the toy poodle, miniature schnauzer, and bichon frise, double two strands of yarn.

GRAFT YARN TO THE BODY & HEAD

01 Insert pins into the back at ⅝" (1.5 cm) intervals.

02 When inserting pins, stagger the alignment for each row. Repeat for as many rows as needed.

03 Insert the needle under one stitch at the pinned area.

04 Pull the yarn through the stitch, leaving about ¾" (2 cm) additional yarn than the noted finished length.

05 Insert the needle back through the same stitch as step 3, creating a backstitch.

06 The yarn can tangle easily. Hold it in place as you pull the yarn through when making the backstitch.

07 Trim the yarn so it matches the length left in step 4.

08 One row of grafting is complete.

09 For the second row, repeat steps 3–7, staggering the backstitches between those of the first row, as marked by the pins.

10 Two rows are now complete. Repeat steps 3–7 and graft yarn to the body and head at ⅝" (1.5 cm) intervals.

GRAFT YARN TO THE FACE, MUZZLE, EARS & LEGS

For the toy poodle and bichon frise, use the same grafting method for these areas as used for the body.

01 Insert pins into the muzzle and legs at ⅜" (1 cm) intervals.

02 Insert the threaded needle under one stitch at the pinned area.

03 Pull the yarn through the stitch, leaving ¾" (2 cm) more yarn than the noted finished length. Trim to the desired finished length.

04 There's no need to make a backstitch when attaching the yarn in these areas.

05 Tangle the yarn by pricking the base of the grafted yarn with a felting needle.

06 Pull the yarn taut to make sure that it cannot easily be removed. It's important that the yarn is secure; otherwise, it may fall out when brushed.

07 For this individual dog, you will change the color of the grafting yarn so the center of the muzzle matches the color of the crocheted body. Repeat steps 2–6 to complete grafting yarn for the muzzle.

Completed view once yarn has been grafted to the entire body.

BRUSH THE GRAFTED YARN

01 Use a slicker brush to loosen the yarn, holding the base of the grafted yarn in place with your finger.

02 Make sure to brush the yarn from different directions.

03 Completed view after all the grafted yarn for the muzzle has been brushed.

HOW TO TRIM THE GRAFTED YARN

01 Trim the grafted yarn to the desired finished length. Don't cut the yarn all at once; trim it gradually, checking the length as you go.

02 If you come across areas of yarn that have not been loosened, stop and brush the yarn before trimming it.

03 Completed view once the muzzle area has been trimmed.

FOR SHORT HAIRED DOGS

Short yarn tends to come off easily after loosening, so prick the base of the grafted yarn again with a felting needle to secure in place.

FOR LONG HAIRED DOGS

Adjust longer yarn as you arrange the flow. A clean cut look around the eyes and above the muzzle creates a realistic expression.

Note: When you brush the yarn, small fibers will fly around, so I recommend wearing a mask to avoid inhaling them.

FINISH THE FACE (FOR SHORT HAIRED DOGS, SUCH AS DACHSHUNDS, PAPILLONS, AND CHIHUAHUAS)

01 Prick the grafted yarn with a felting needle along the flow of fur.

02 Tangle all the yarn along the shape of the muzzle.

03 The muzzle fur is now more compacted. Follow the same process to graft, brush, and trim the fur on the rest of the face.

HOW TO MAKE EYEBROWS

Make long straight stitches following the placement noted in the photo. Take care not to pull the yarn too tight as you draw it through. Use a brush to loosen the yarn, and then use a felting needle to adjust the flow. Cut the loops at the ends of the eyebrows, and then give them another brush to help blend with the rest of the fur on the face.

Out = Position to draw the needle out
In = Position to insert the needle

Note: Use a needle felting claw to loosen and arrange the yarn around the eye buttons.

HOW TO HANDLE AREAS WITHOUT GRAFTING

The belly area (left) doesn't need to be grafted for the stand and lie down poses, since it's not visible.

For the sit pose (left), do not graft the belly area between the front and back legs, or the bottom area.

Note: If you don't like seeing the crocheted surface, use a slicker brush to make the yarn a bit more fuzzy or graft short yarns to these areas.

HOW TO MAKE EARS WITH WRAPPED YARN

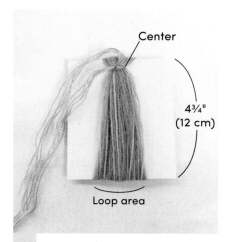

Center

4¾" (12 cm)

Loop area

01 Wrap yarn around a 4¾" (12 cm) piece of cardboard 30 times. Tie a doubled 19¾" (50 cm) long yarn to the wrapped yarn near the top.

Note: Use a 5½" (14 cm) piece of cardboard for the dachshund.

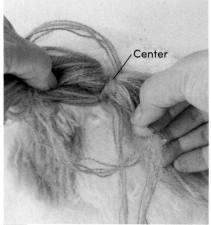

Center

02 Cut the looped area at the bottom. Thread the yarn that was tied to the wrapped yarn onto a needle and use it to sew the ear to the head. Do the same for the other end of the yarn and then make knot under the ear.

03 Arrange the yarn as desired, then use a felting needle to adjust the shape of the ear.

Toy Poodle / Sit

TOOLS & MATERIALS

- J/10 (6 mm) crochet hook
- 421 yards (320 g) bulky weight acrylic yarn in mocha
- Pair of 15 mm black plastic toy safety eyes
- One 18 mm black plastic toy safety nose
- Polyester fiber fill toy stuffing (about 50 g)
- Stitch marker
- Yarn needle
- Felting needle
- Slicker brush

YARN COMBINATION CHART

Area	Yarn Used		Yarn Color	Amount	Strands
Crocheting the Foundation	A	Bulky weight acrylic	Mocha	289 yds (220 g)	2 strands
Grafting the Fur	B	Bulky weight acrylic	Mocha	132 yds (100 g)	2 strands

CONSTRUCTION STEPS

1. Crochet the body, head, front legs, back legs, ears, muzzle, and tail following instructions on pages 62–64 (also see pages 45–52).

2. Stuff and assemble the body parts following the instructions for the sit pose on pages 53–55.

3. Graft yarn according to the lengths listed on page 65 (refer to pages 56–58 for general grafting instructions).

4. Follow the techniques on page 58 to loosen the yarn and trim the fur into shape. Use the photos below as a reference.

Front   Side   Back

CROCHET INSTRUCTIONS

Crochet Symbol Key

★ = magic ring   ∧ = ⋀ = sc2tog   ⋁ = sc3 in next st

0 = ch st   ∨ = ⋎ = sc2 in next st   ⋓ = sc5 in next st

• = slst

Body (make 1)

With Yarn A, make a magic ring.

Rnd 1: ch1 (does not count as a st throughout), sc6 in magic ring, slst in beg ch1 [6]

Place stitch marker in first st of rnd 1 and move it up after each round

Rnd 2: ch1, (sc2 in next st) 6 times, slst in beg ch1 [12]

Rnd 3: ch1, (sc1, sc2 in next st) 6 times, slst in beg ch1 [18]

Rnd 4: ch1, (sc2, sc2 in next st) 6 times, slst in beg ch1 [24]

Rnd 5: ch1, sc2 in first st, sc22, sc2 in last st, slst in beg ch1 [26]

Rnds 6–9: ch1, sc1 in each st, slst in beg ch1 (4 rnds)

Rnd 10: ch1, sc1, sc2tog, sc20, sc2tog, sc1, slst beg ch1 [24]

Rnd 11: ch1, sc1 in each st, slst in beg ch1

Rnd 12: ch1, sc1, sc2tog, sc18, sc2tog, sc1, slst in beg ch1 [22]

Rnd 13: ch1, sc1 in each st, slst in beg ch1

Rnd 14: ch1, sc1, sc2tog, sc5, sc2 in next st, sc4, sc2 in next st, sc5, sc2tog, sc1, slst in beg ch1 [22]

Rnds 15–18: ch1, sc1 in each st, slst in beg ch1 (4 rnds)

Rnd 19: as rnd 14

Rnds 20–22: ch1, sc1 in each st, slst in beg ch1 (3 rnds)

Rnd 23: ch1, sc1, (sc2tog, sc4) 3 times, sc2tog, sc1, slst in beg ch1 [18]

Fasten off.

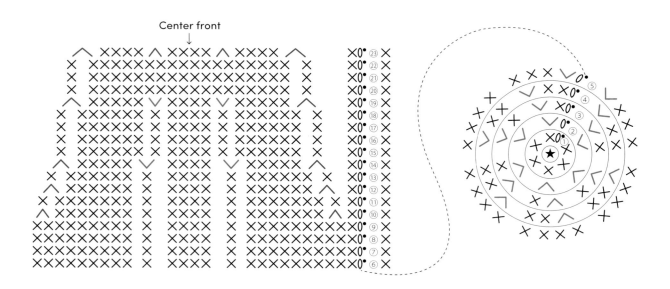

Center front

Head (make 1)

With Yarn A, make a magic ring.

Rnd 1: ch1 (does not count as a st throughout), sc6 in magic ring, slst in beg ch1 [6]

Place stitch marker in first st of rnd 1 and move it up after each round

Rnd 2: ch1, (sc2 in next st) 6 times, slst in beg ch1 [12]

Rnd 3: ch1, (sc1, sc2 in next st) 6 times, slst in beg ch1 [18]

Rnd 4: ch1, (sc2, sc2 in next st) 6 times, slst in beg ch1 [24]

Rnds 5–9: ch1, sc1 in each st, slst in beg ch1 (5 rnds)

Rnd 10: ch1, sc8, sc2tog, sc4, sc2tog, sc8, slst in beg ch1 [22]

Rnd 11: ch1, sc4, (sc2tog, sc2) 3 times, sc2tog, sc4, slst in beg ch1 [18]

Rnd 12: ch1, sc1 in each st, slst in beg ch1

Fasten off.

Attach toy safety eyes to front of face at position shown in diagram on page 65, between rnds 6 and 7, leaving 5 sts between eyes.

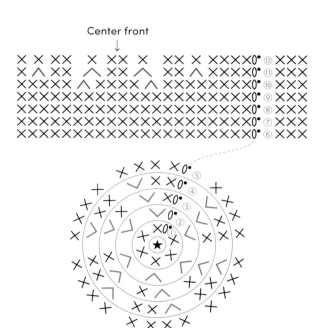

Center front

Front Legs (make 2)

With Yarn A, make a magic ring.

Rnd 1: ch1 (does not count as a st throughout), sc7 in magic ring, slst in beg ch1 [7]

Place stitch marker in first st of rnd 1 and move it up after each round

Rnds 2–8: ch1, sc1 in each st, slst in beg ch1 (7 rnds)

Rnd 9: ch1, sc6, sc2 in last st, slst in beg ch1 [8]

Rnd 10: ch1, sc1 in each st, slst in beg ch1

Rnd 11: ch1, sc7, sc2 in last st, slst in beg ch1 [9]

Rnd 12: ch1, sc8, sc2 in last st, slst in beg ch1 [10]

Rnd 13: ch1, sc9, sc2 in last st, slst in beg ch1 [11]

Fasten off.

Back Legs (make 2)

With Yarn A, make a magic ring.

Rnd 1: ch1 (does not count as a st throughout), sc7 in magic ring, slst in beg ch1 [7]

Place stitch marker in first st of rnd 1 and move it up after each round

Rnds 2–7: ch1, sc1 in each st, slst in beg ch1 (6 rnds)

Rnd 8: ch1, sc3, sc5 in next st, sc3, slst in beg ch1 [11]

Rnd 9: ch1, sc5, sc5 in next st, sc5, slst in beg ch1 [15]

Rnd 10: ch1, sc7, sc3 in next st, sc7, slst in beg ch1 [17]

Rnds 11–12: ch1, sc1 in each st, slst in beg ch1 (2 rnds)

Rnd 13: ch1, sc6, sc2tog, sc1, sc2tog, sc6, slst in beg ch1

Fasten off.

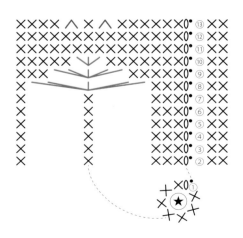

Ears (make 2)

With Yarn A, make 4ch, leaving a 12" (30 cm) tail of yarn.

Work in rows.

Row 1: sc1 in second ch from hook, sc1 in each remaining ch, turn [3]

Row 2: ch1 (does not count as a st throughout), sc2 in first st, sc1, sc2 in last st, turn [5]

Rows 3–4: ch1, sc1 in each st to end, turn (2 rows)

Fasten off.

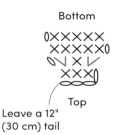

Bottom

Top

Leave a 12" (30 cm) tail

Muzzle (make 1)

With Yarn A, make 5ch.

Rnd 1: skip first ch, sc1 in next ch, sc1 in next 2 ch, sc3 in last ch, rotate and work along opposite side of chain, sc1 in next 2 ch, sc2 in last ch, slst in skipped ch at beg of rnd [10]

Place stitch marker in first st of rnd 1 and move it up after each round

Rnd 2: ch1, (sc4, sc2 in next st) twice, slst in beg ch1 [12]

Rnds 3–4: ch1, sc1 in each st, slst in beg ch1 (2 rnds)

Fasten off.

Add toy safety nose at position shown in diagram, at center front of muzzle, between rnds 1 and 2.

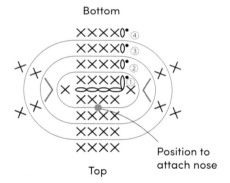

Bottom

Top

Position to attach nose

Tail (make 1)

With Yarn A, make a magic ring.

Rnd 1: ch1 (does not count as a st throughout), sc5 in magic ring, slst in beg ch1 [5]

Place stitch marker in first st of rnd 1 and move it up after each round

Rnd 2: ch1, sc4, sc2 in last st, slst in beg ch1 [6]

Rnds 3–7: ch1, sc1 in each st, slst in beg ch1 (5 rnds)

Fasten off.

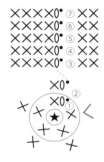

12" (30 cm) tall x 8" (20 cm) long

Location	Yarn Length
Head	¾" (2 cm)
Body	1¼"-2" (3–5 cm)
Tail	2" (5 cm)
Muzzle	¾" (2 cm)
Legs	¾" (2 cm)
Ears	2¾"–4¾" (7–12 cm)

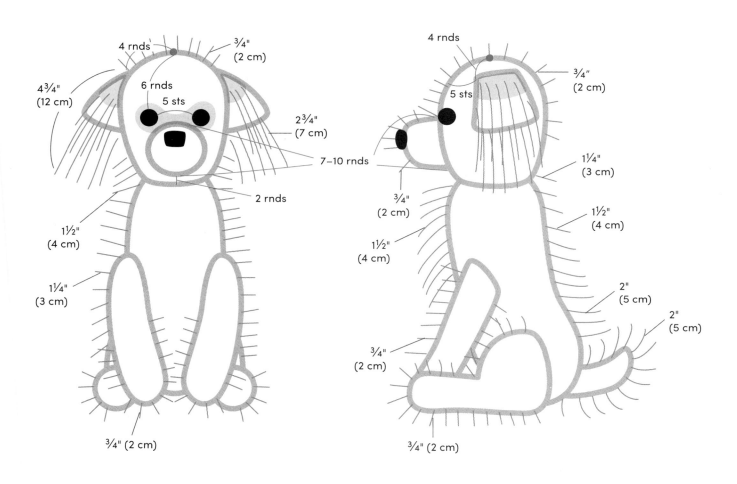

 • For grafting, use two strands of acrylic bulky yarn.
- Do not graft yarn at the base of the ear. Start slightly below the base and graft layers of yarn downward to create volume at the bottom of the ear.
- Brush and trim the yarn until you achieve the desired shape.
- ▨ = Needle felt the areas shaded in light blue in order to compress the yarn.

TOOLS & MATERIALS

- J/10 (6 mm) crochet hook
- 421 yards (320 g) bulky weight acrylic yarn in beige
- Pair of 15 mm black plastic toy safety eyes
- One 18 mm black plastic toy safety nose
- Polyester fiber fill toy stuffing (about 50 g)
- Stitch marker
- Yarn needle
- Felting needle
- Slicker brush

YARN COMBINATION CHART

Area	Yarn Used		Yarn Color	Amount	Strands
Crocheting the Foundation	A	Bulky weight acrylic	Beige	289 yds (220 g)	2 strands
Grafting the Fur	B	Bulky weight acrylic	Beige	132 yds (100 g)	2 strands

CONSTRUCTION STEPS

1. Crochet the body, head, front legs, back legs, ears, muzzle, and tail following instructions on pages 67–69 (also see pages 45–52).

2. Stuff and assemble the body parts following the instructions for the stand pose on pages 54–55.

3. Graft yarn according to the lengths listed on page 70 (refer to pages 56–58 for general grafting instructions).

4. Follow the techniques on page 58 to loosen the yarn and trim the fur into shape. Use the photos below as a reference.

Front   Side   Back

CROCHET INSTRUCTIONS

Crochet Symbol Key

★ = magic ring ∧ = ⩕ = sc2tog ⋁ = sc3 in next st

0 = ch st ⋁ = ⋎ = sc2 in next st ⋓ = sc5 in next st

• = slst

Body (make 1)

With Yarn A, make a magic ring.

Rnd 1: ch1 (does not count as a st throughout), sc6 in magic ring, slst in beg ch1 [6]

Place stitch marker in first st of rnd 1 and move it up after each round.

Rnd 2: ch1, (sc2 in next st) 6 times, slst in beg ch1 [12]

Rnd 3: ch1, (sc1, sc2 in next st) 6 times, slst in beg ch1 [18]

Rnd 4: ch1, (sc2, sc2 in next st) 6 times, slst in beg ch1 [24]

Rnds 5–24: ch1, sc1 in each st, slst in beg ch1 (20 rnds)

Rnd 25: ch1, (sc2, sc2tog) 6 times, slst in beg ch1 [18]

Begin to stuff body firmly.

Rnd 26: ch1, (sc1, sc2tog) 6 times, slst in beg ch1 [12]

Rnd 27: ch1, (sc2tog) 6 times, slst in beg ch1 [6]

Fasten off leaving a long tail end. Add more stuffing if needed then thread yarn through stitches of last round and pull tightly to close.

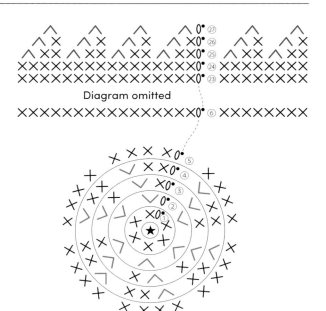

Diagram omitted

Head (make 1)

With Yarn A, make a magic ring.

Rnd 1: ch1 (does not count as a st throughout), sc6 in magic ring, slst in beg ch1 [6]

Place stitch marker in first st of rnd 1 and move it up after each round

Rnd 2: ch1, (sc2 in next st) 6 times, slst in beg ch1 [12]

Rnd 3: ch1, (sc1, sc2 in next st) 6 times, slst in beg ch1 [18]

Rnd 4: ch1, (sc2, sc2 in next st) 6 times, slst in beg ch1 [24]

Rnds 5–9: ch1, sc1 in each st, slst in beg ch1 (5 rnds)

Rnd 10: ch1, sc8, sc2tog, sc4, sc2tog, sc8, slst in beg ch1 [22]

Rnd 11: ch1, sc4, (sc2tog, sc2) 3 times, sc2tog, sc4, slst in beg ch1 [18]

Rnd 12: ch1, sc1 in each st, slst in beg ch1

Fasten off.

Attach toy safety eyes to front of face at position shown in diagram on page 70, between rnds 6 and 7, leaving 5 sts between eyes.

Center front
↓

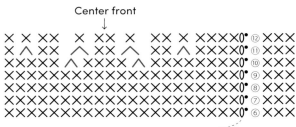

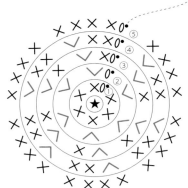

Front Legs (make 2)

With Yarn A, make a magic ring.

Rnd 1: ch1 (does not count as a st throughout), sc8 in magic ring, slst in beg ch1 [8]

Place stitch marker in first st of rnd 1 and move it up after each round

Rnds 2–9: ch1, sc1 in each st, slst in beg ch1 (8 rnds)

Rnd 10: ch1, sc7, sc2 in next st, slst in beg ch1 [9]

Rnd 11: ch1, sc8, sc2 in next st, slst in beg ch1 [10]

Rnd 12: ch1, sc9, sc2 in next st, slst in beg ch1 [11]

Fasten off.

Back Legs (make 2)

With Yarn A, make a magic ring.

Rnd 1: ch1 (does not count as a st throughout), sc8 in magic ring, slst in beg ch1 [8]

Place stitch marker in first st of rnd 1 and move it up after each round

Rnds 2–6: ch1, sc1 in each st, slst in beg ch1 (5 rnds)

Rnd 7: ch1, sc7, sc2 in next st, slst in beg ch1 [9]

Rnd 8: ch1, sc8, sc2 in next st, slst in beg ch1 [10]

Rnd 9: ch1, sc9, sc2 in next st, slst in beg ch1 [11]

Rnd 10: ch1, sc10, sc2 in next st, slst in beg ch1 [12]

Rnd 11: ch1, sc11, sc2 in next st, slst in beg ch1 [13]

Fasten off.

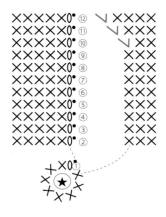

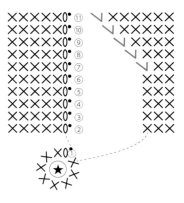

Ears (make 2)

With Yarn A, make 4ch, leaving a 12" (30 cm) tail of yarn.

Work in rows.

Row 1: sc1 in second ch from hook, sc1 in each remaining ch, turn [3]

Row 2: ch1 (does not count as a st throughout), sc2 in first st, sc1, sc2 in last st, turn [5]

Rows 3–4: ch1, sc1 in each st to end, turn

Fasten off.

Bottom

Top

Leave a
12" (30 cm)
tail

Muzzle (make 1)

With Yarn A, make 5ch.
Rnd 1: skip first ch, sc1 in next ch, sc1 in next 2 ch, sc3 in last ch, rotate and work along opposite side of chain, sc1 in next 2 ch, sc2 in last ch, slst in skipped ch at beg of rnd [10]
Place stitch marker in first st of rnd 1 and move it up after each round.
Rnd 2: ch1, (sc4, sc2 in next st) twice, slst in beg ch1 [12]
Rnds 3–4: ch1, sc1 in each st, slst in beg ch1 (2 rnds)
Fasten off.
Add toy safety nose at position shown in diagram, at center front of muzzle, between rnds 1 and 2.

Tail (make 1)

With Yarn A, make a magic ring.
Rnd 1: ch1 (does not count as a st throughout), sc5 in magic ring, slst in beg ch1 [5]
Place stitch marker in first st of rnd 1 and move it up after each round
Rnd 2: ch1, sc4, sc2 in next st, slst in beg ch1 [6]
Rnds 3–7: ch1, sc1 in each st, slst in beg ch1 (5 rnds)
Fasten off.

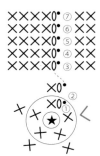

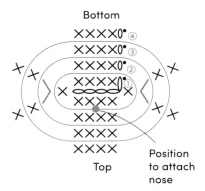

Bottom

Top

Position to attach nose

Location	Yarn Length
Head	1¼" (3 cm)
Body	1¼"–1½" (3–3.5 cm)
Tail	1¼" (3 cm)
Muzzle	1" (2.5 cm)
Legs	1" (2.5 cm)
Ears	2" (5 cm)

10¾" (27 cm) tall × 11¾" (30 cm) long

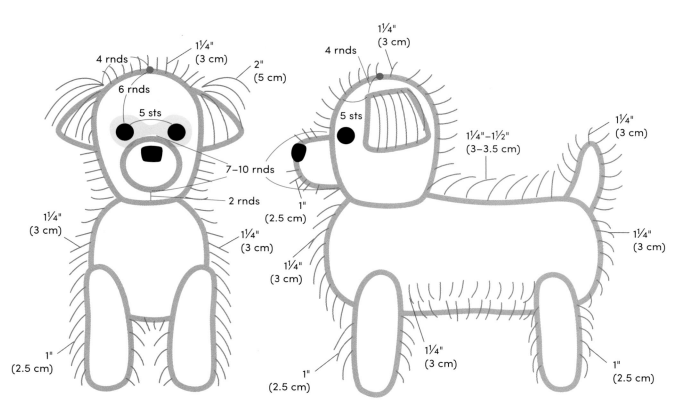

- For grafting, use two strands of acrylic bulky yarn.
- Do not graft yarn on the paws because it will make it difficult for the dog to stand.
- Brush and trim the yarn until you achieve the desired shape.
- ▢ = Needle felt the areas shaded in light blue in order to compress the yarn.

TOOLS & MATERIALS

- I/9 (5.5 mm) crochet hook
- 105 yards (80 g) bulky weight acrylic yarn in white
- 27 yds (20 g) bulky weight acrylic yarn in dark beige
- 255 yds (65 g) sport weight acrylic yarn in white
- 119 yds (30 g) sport weight acrylic yarn in golden brown
- 175 yds (40 g) of light fingering weight acrylic/mohair blend yarn in white
- 88 yards (20 g) of light fingering weight acrylic/mohair blend yarn in brown

- Pair of 15 mm black plastic toy safety eyes
- One 21 mm black plastic toy safety nose
- Polyester fiber fill toy stuffing (about 40 g)
- Stitch marker
- Yarn needle
- Felting needle
- Slicker brush

YARN COMBINATION CHART

Area		Yarn Used	Yarn Color	Amount	Strands
Crocheting the Foundation	A	Bulky weight acrylic	White	105 yds (80 g)	1 strand
		Sport weight acrylic	White	99 yds (25 g)	1 strand
	B	Bulky weight acrylic	Dark beige	27 yds (20 g)	1 strand
		Sport weight acrylic	Golden brown	40 yds (10 g)	1 strand
Grafting the Fur	C	Sport weight acrylic	White	156 yds (40 g)	2 strands
		Light fingering weight acrylic/mohair blend	White	175 yds (40 g)	2 strands
	D	Sport weight acrylic	Golden brown	79 yds (20 g)	2 strands
		Light fingering weight acrylic/mohair blend	Brown	88 yds (20 g)	2 strands

CONSTRUCTION STEPS

1. Crochet the body, head, front legs, back legs, ears, muzzle, and tail following instructions on pages 72–74 (also see pages 45–52).

2. Stuff and assemble the body parts following the instructions for the sit pose on pages 53–55.

3. Graft yarn according to the lengths listed on page 75 (refer to pages 56–58 for general grafting instructions).

4. Follow the techniques on page 58 to loosen the yarn and trim the fur into shape. Use the photos at right as a reference.

Front   Side   Back

CROCHET INSTRUCTIONS

Crochet Symbol Key

★ = magic ring

0 = ch st

• = slst

∧ = ⋀ = sc2tog

∨ = ⋎ = sc2 in next st

⋓ = 5 single crochet increase

⫯ = Cluster stitch variation with 3 half double crochet (refer to page 52)

Yarn Color Key

□ = Yarn A

▨ = Yarn B

Body (make 1)

With Yarn A, make a magic ring.

Rnd 1: ch1 (does not count as a st throughout), sc6 in magic ring, slst in beg ch1 [6]

Place stitch marker in first st of rnd 1 and move it up after each round

Rnd 2: ch1, (sc2 in next st) 6 times, slst in beg ch1 [12]

Rnd 3: ch1, (sc1, sc2 in next st) 6 times, slst in beg ch1 [18]

Rnd 4: ch1, (sc2, sc2 in next st) 6 times, slst in beg ch1 [24]

Rnd 5: ch1, sc2 in first st, sc22, sc2 in next st, slst in beg ch1 [26]

Rnds 6–9: ch1, sc1 in each st, slst in beg ch1 (4 rnds)

Rnd 10: ch1, sc1, sc2tog, sc20, sc2tog, sc1, slst in beg ch1 [24]

Rnd 11: ch1, sc1 in each st, slst in beg ch1

Rnd 12: ch1, sc1, sc2tog, sc18, sc2tog, sc1, slst in beg ch1 [22]

Rnd 13: ch1, sc1 in each st, slst in beg ch1

Rnd 14: ch1, sc1, sc2tog, sc5, sc2 in next st, sc4, sc2 in next st, sc5, sc2tog, sc1, slst in beg ch1 [22]

Rnds 15–18: ch1, sc1 in each st, slst in beg ch1 (4 rnds)

Rnd 19: as rnd 14

Rnds 20–22: ch1, sc1 in each st, slst in beg ch1 (3 rnds)

Rnd 23: ch1, sc1, (sc2tog, sc4) 3 times, sc2tog, sc1, slst in beg ch1 [18]

Fasten off.

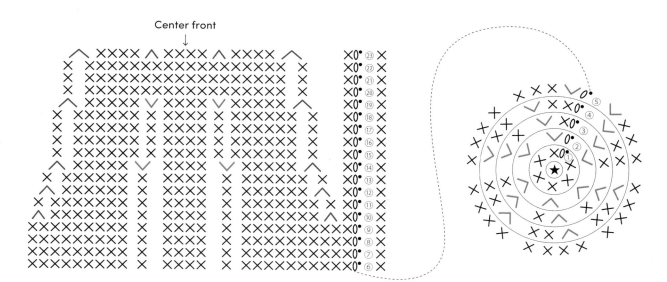

Head (make 1)

With Yarn A, make a magic ring.
Rnd 1: ch1 (does not count as a st throughout), sc6 in magic ring, slst in beg ch1 [6]
Place stitch marker in first st of rnd 1 and move it up after each round
Rnd 2: ch1, (sc2 in next st) 6 times, slst in beg ch1 [12]
Rnd 3: ch1, (sc1, sc2 in next st) 6 times, slst in beg ch1 [18]
Rnd 4: ch1, (sc2, sc2 in next st) 6 times, slst in beg ch1 [24]
Rnd 5: ch1, sc2, sc2 in next st, sc2, in Yarn B sc1, sc2 in next st, sc2, in Yarn A (sc1, sc2 in next st, sc1) twice, in Yarn B sc2, sc2 in next st, sc1, in Yarn A sc2, sc2 in next st, sc2, slst in beg ch1 [30]
Rnds 6–7: in Yarn A ch1, sc6, in Yarn B sc7, in Yarn A sc4, in Yarn B sc7, in Yarn A sc6, slst in beg ch1 (2 rnds)
Rnds 8–9: in Yarn A ch1, sc6, in Yarn B sc8, in Yarn A sc2, in Yarn B sc8, in Yarn A sc6, slst in beg ch1 (2 rnds)
Rnd 10: in Yarn A ch1, sc6, in Yarn B sc7, in Yarn A sc4, in Yarn B sc7, in Yarn A sc6, slst in beg ch1
Rnd 11: in Yarn A ch1, sc4, sc2tog, in Yarn B sc3, sc2tog, sc1, in Yarn A sc2, sc2tog, sc2, in Yarn B sc1, sc2tog, sc3, in Yarn A sc2tog, sc4, slst in beg ch1 [25]
Continue in Yarn A only
Rnd 12: ch1, sc8, sc2tog, sc5, sc2tog, sc8, slst in beg ch1 [23]
Rnd 13: ch1, sc3, (sc2tog, sc2) 5 times, slst in beg ch1 [18]
Rnd 14: ch1, sc1 in each st, slst in beg ch1
Fasten off.
Attach toy safety eyes to front of face at position shown in diagram on page 75, between rnds 8 and 9, leaving 6 sts between eyes.

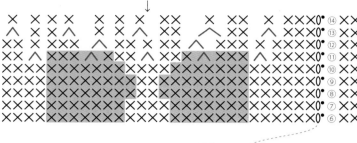

Center front

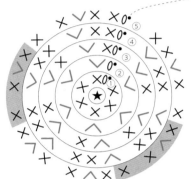

Muzzle (make 1)

With Yarn A, make 5ch.
Rnd 1: skip first ch, sc1 in next ch, sc1 in next 2 ch, sc3 in last ch, rotate and work along opposite side of chain, sc1 in next 2 ch, sc2 in last ch, slst in skipped ch at beg of rnd [10]
Place stitch marker in first st of rnd 1 and move it up after each round
Rnd 2: ch1, (sc4, sc2 in next st) twice, slst in beg ch1 [12]
Rnd 3: ch1, sc7, sc2 in next 2 sts, sc3, slst in beg ch1 [14]
Fasten off.
Add toy safety nose at position shown in diagram, at center front of muzzle, between rnds 1 and 2.

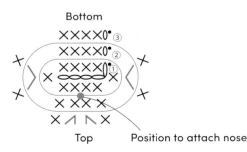

Bottom

Top   Position to attach nose

Tail (make 1)

With Yarn A, make a magic ring.
Rnd 1: ch1 (does not count as a st throughout), sc5 in magic ring, slst in beg ch 1 [5]
Place stitch marker in first st of rnd 1 and move it up after each round
Rnd 2: ch1, sc4, sc2 in next st, slst in beg ch1 [6]
Rnds 3–7: ch1, sc1 in each st, slst in beg ch1 (5 rnds)
Fasten off.

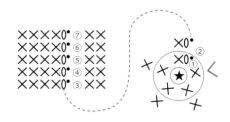

Front Legs (make 2)

With Yarn A, make a magic ring.

Rnd 1: ch1 (does not count as a st throughout), sc8 in magic ring, slst in beg ch1 [8]

Place stitch marker in first st of rnd 1 and move it up after each round

Rnd 2: ch1, sc2, 3hdc-cl in each of next 4 sts, sc2, slst in beg ch1

Rnds 3–8: ch1, sc1 in each st, slst in beg ch1 (6 rnds)

Rnd 9: ch1, sc7, sc2 in last st, slst in beg ch1 [9]

Rnd 10: ch1, sc1 in each st, slst in beg ch1

Rnd 11: ch1, sc8, sc2 in last st, slst in beg ch1 [10]

Rnd 12: ch1, sc9, sc2 in last st, slst in beg ch1 [11]

Rnd 13: ch1, sc10, sc2 in last st, slst in beg ch1 [12]

Fasten off.

Back Legs (make 2)

With Yarn A, make a magic ring.

Rnd 1: ch1 (does not count as a st throughout), sc8 in magic ring, slst in beg ch1 [8]

Place stitch marker in first st of rnd 1 and move it up after each round

Rnd 2: ch1, sc2, 3hdc-cl in each of next 4 sts, sc2, slst in beg ch1

Rnds 3–8: ch1, sc1 in each st, slst in beg ch1 (6 rnds)

Rnd 9: ch1, sc7, sc2 in last st, slst in beg ch1 [9]

Rnd 10: ch1, sc4, sc5 in next st, sc4, slst in beg ch1 [13]

Rnd 11: ch1, sc6, sc5 in next st, sc6, slst in beg ch1 [17]

Rnds 12–14: ch1, sc1 in each st, slst in beg ch1 (3 rnds)

Rnd 15: ch1, sc5, sc2tog, sc3, sc2tog, sc5, slst in beg ch1 [15]

Fasten off.

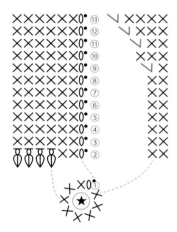

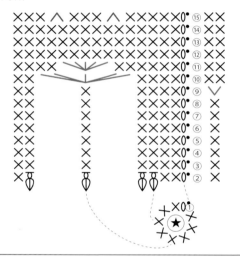

Ears (make 2)

With Yarn B, make a magic ring.

Rnd 1: ch1 (does not count as a st throughout), sc5 in magic ring, slst in beg ch1 [5]

Place stitch marker in first st of rnd 1 and move it up after each round

Rnd 2: in Yarn B ch1, sc2 in first st, (in Yarn A sc2 in next st, in Yarn B sc2 in next st) twice, slst in beg ch1 [10]

Rnd 3: in Yarn B ch1, sc2 in first st, in Yarn A sc3, in Yarn B sc2, in Yarn A sc3, in Yarn B sc2 in next st, slst in beg ch1 [12]

Rnd 4: in Yarn B ch1, sc2 in first st, in Yarn A sc4, in Yarn B sc2, in Yarn A sc4, in Yarn B sc2 in next st, slst in beg ch1 [14]

Rnd 5: in Yarn B ch1, sc2 in first st, in Yarn A sc5, in Yarn B sc2, in Yarn A sc5, in Yarn B sc2 in next st, slst in beg ch1 [16]

Rnd 6: in Yarn B ch1, sc2 in first st, in Yarn A sc6, in Yarn B sc2, in Yarn A sc6, in Yarn B sc2 in next st, slst in beg ch1 [18]

Rnd 7: in Yarn B ch1, sc2 in first st, in Yarn A sc7, in Yarn B sc2, in Yarn A sc7, in Yarn B sc2 in next st, slst in beg ch1 [20]

Rnd 8: in Yarn B ch1, sc2 in first st, in Yarn A sc8, in Yarn B sc2, in Yarn A sc8, in Yarn B sc2 in next st, slst in beg ch1 [22]

To make second ear, switch the colors, using Yarn A instead of Yarn B and vice versa.

Right ear: Yarn A
Left ear: Yarn B

Right ear: Yarn B
Left ear: Yarn A

Inside center

GRAFTING & FINISHING

Location	Yarn Used	Yarn Length
Head	C, D	⅝"–3⅛" (1.5–8 cm)
Body	C, D	2½"–3⅛" (6–8 cm)
Tail	C	2¾" (7 cm)
Muzzle	C	⅝" (1.5 cm)
Legs	C	2" (5 cm) (at base only)
Ears	D	3½" (9 cm)

FINISHED SIZE

10¾" (27 cm) tall × 7" (18 cm) long

How to Graft the Ears

Prepare pieces of yarn that are at least twice the desired finished length (about 8" [20 cm] long). Use backstitch to attach the yarn one row at a time along the contour of the ear (refer to page 57). Once the yarn has been attached, loosen the yarn and adjust the flow using a felting needle.

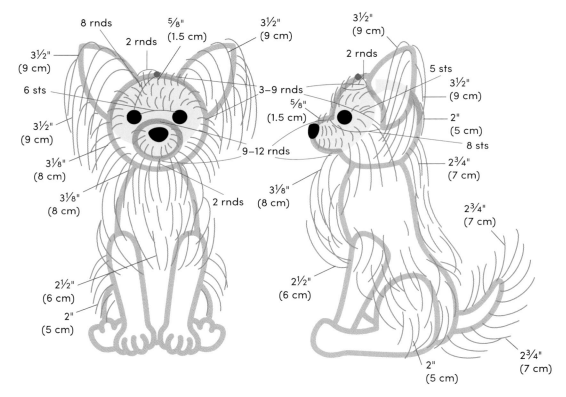

- For grafting, always use a total of 4 strands (2 of the sport weight acrylic and 2 of the light fingering weight acrylic/mohair blend).
- Attach the ears so that the front side is white.
- Brush the front and back with a slicker brush before grafting the ears.
- When grafting the yarn to the face, use the same yarn colors used to crochet the head (refer to the crochet chart on page 73 for color placement).
- Graft Yarn D to the back of the body and the base of the tail as desired.
- Graft yarn to the legs only in the areas where they attach to the body. Do not graft yarn to the paws.
- ⬜ = Needle felt the areas shaded in light blue in order to compress the yarn and shape the head.

TOOLS & MATERIALS

- H/8 (5 mm) crochet hook
- 105 yards (80 g) bulky weight acrylic yarn in beige
- 79 yds (60 g) bulky weight acrylic yarn in white
- 158 yds (40 g) sport weight acrylic yarn in light beige
- 79 yds (20 g) sport weight acrylic yarn in white
- 175 yds (40 g) of light fingering weight acrylic/mohair blend yarn in cream

- 88 yards (20 g) of light fingering weight acrylic/mohair blend yarn in white
- Pair of 18 mm black plastic toy safety eyes
- One 21 mm black plastic toy safety nose
- Polyester fiber fill toy stuffing (about 40 g)
- Stitch marker
- Yarn needle
- Felting needle
- Slicker brush

YARN COMBINATION CHART

Use		Yarn Type	Yarn Color	Strands
Crocheting the Foundation	A	Bulky weight acrylic	Beige	1 strand
	B	Bulky weight acrylic	White	1 strand
Grafting the Fur	C	Sport weight acrylic	Light beige	2 strands
		Light fingering weight acrylic/mohair blend	Cream	2 strands
	D	Sport weight acrylic	White	2 strands
		Light fingering weight acrylic/mohair blend	White	2 strands

CONSTRUCTION STEPS

1. Crochet the body, head, front legs, back legs, ears, muzzle, and tail following instructions on pages 77–79 (also see pages 45–52).

2. Stuff and assemble the body parts following the instructions for the lie down pose on pages 54–55.

3. Graft yarn according to the lengths listed on page 80 (refer to pages 56–58 for general grafting instructions).

4. Follow the techniques on page 58 to loosen the yarn and trim the fur into shape. Use the photos below as a reference.

Front

Side

Back

CROCHET INSTRUCTIONS

Crochet Symbol Key

★ = magic ring

0 = ch st

• = slst

∧ = ⋏ = sc2tog

∨ = ⋎ = sc2 in next st

∀ = 3 single crochet increase

⋓ = 5 single crochet increase

⍦ = Cluster stitch variation with 3 half double crochet (refer to page 52)

Yarn Color Key

▨ = Yarn A

☐ = Yarn B

Body (make 1)

With Yarn B, make a magic ring.

Rnd 1: ch1 (does not count as a st throughout), sc6 in magic ring, slst in beg ch1 [6]

Place stitch marker in first st of rnd 1 and move it up after each round

Rnd 2: ch1, (sc2 in next st) 6 times, slst in beg ch1 [12]

Rnd 3: ch1, (sc1, sc2 in next st) 6 times, slst in beg ch1 [18]

Rnd 4: in Yarn A ch1, (sc2, sc2 in next st) twice, in Yarn B (sc2, sc2 in next st) twice, in Yarn A (sc2, sc2 in next st) twice, slst in beg ch1 [24]

Rnds 5–24: in Yarn A ch1, sc7, in Yarn B sc10, in Yarn A sc7, slst in beg ch1 (20 rnds)

Rnd 25: in Yarn A ch1, (sc2, sc2tog) twice, in Yarn B (sc2, sc2tog) twice, in Yarn A (sc2, sc2tog) twice, slst in beg ch1 [18]

Begin to stuff body firmly. Continue in Yarn B only.

Rnd 26: ch1, (sc1, sc2tog) 6 times, slst in beg ch1 [12]

Rnd 27: ch1, (sc2tog) 6 times, slst in beg ch1 [6]

Fasten off leaving a long tail end. Add more stuffing if needed then thread yarn through stitches of last round and pull tightly to close.

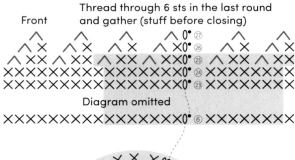

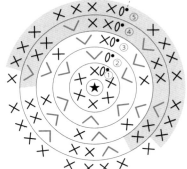

Head (make 1)

With Yarn A, make a magic ring.

Rnd 1: ch1 (does not count as a st throughout), sc6 in magic ring, slst in beg ch1 [6]

Place stitch marker in first st of rnd 1 and move it up after each round

Rnd 2: ch1, (sc2 in next st) 6 times, slst in beg ch1 [12]

Rnd 3: ch1, (sc1, sc2 in next st) 6 times, slst in beg ch1 [18]

Rnd 4: ch1, (sc2, sc2 in next st) 6 times, slst in beg ch1 [24]

Rnd 5: ch1, (sc3, sc2 in next st) 6 times, slst in beg ch1 [30]

Rnd 6: in Yarn A ch1, sc11, in Yarn B sc2, in Yarn A sc4, in Yarn B sc2, in Yarn A sc11, slst in beg ch1

Rnd 7: in Yarn A ch1, sc10, in Yarn B sc4, in Yarn A sc2, in Yarn B sc4, in Yarn A sc10, slst in beg ch1

Rnds 8–10: in Yarn A ch1, sc10, in Yarn B sc10, in Yarn A sc10, slst in beg ch1 (3 rnds)

Rnd 11: in Yarn A ch1, sc2, sc2tog, sc3, sc2tog, sc1, in Yarn B sc1, sc2tog, sc4, sc2tog, sc1, in Yarn A sc1, sc2tog, sc3, sc2tog, sc2, slst in beg ch1 [24]

Rnd 12: in Yarn A ch1, sc8, in Yarn B sc2tog, sc4, sc2tog, in Yarn A sc8, slst in beg ch1 [22]

Rnd 13: in Yarn A ch1, sc4, sc2tog, sc2, in Yarn B sc2tog, sc2, sc2tog, in Yarn A sc2, sc2tog, sc4, slst in beg ch1 [18]

Rnd 14: In Yarn A, ch1, sc7, in Yarn B sc4, in Yarn A sc7, slst in beg ch1. Fasten off.

Attach toy safety eyes to front of face at position shown in diagram on page 80, between rnds 8 and 9, leaving 6 sts between eyes.

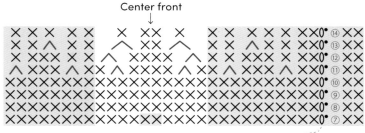

Center front

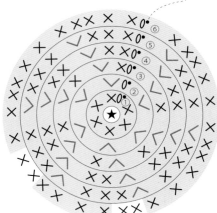

Muzzle (make 1)

With Yarn B, make 5ch.

Rnd 1: skip first ch, sc1 in next ch, sc1 in next 2 ch, sc3 in last ch, rotate and work along opposite side of chain, sc1 in next 2 ch, sc2 in last ch, slst in skipped ch at beg of rnd [10]

Place stitch marker in first st of rnd 1 and move it up after each round

Rnd 2: ch1, (sc4, sc2 in next st) twice, slst in beg ch1 [12]

Rnd 3: ch1, sc1 in each st, slst in beg ch1
Fasten off.

Add toy safety nose at position shown in diagram, at center front of muzzle, between rnds 1 and 2.

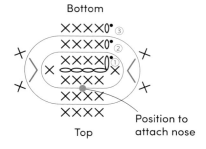

Bottom

Top

Position to attach nose

Tail (make 1)

With Yarn A, make a magic ring.

Rnd 1: ch1 (does not count as a st throughout), sc5 in magic ring, slst in beg ch1 [5]

Place stitch marker in first st of rnd 1 and move it up after each round

Rnd 2: ch1, sc4, sc2 in last st, slst in beg ch1 [6]

Rnds 3–7: ch1, sc1 in each st, slst in beg ch1 (5 rnds)
Fasten off.

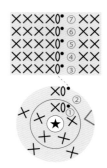

Front Legs (make 2)

With Yarn B, make a magic ring.

Rnd 1: ch1 (does not count as a st throughout), sc8 in magic ring, slst in beg ch1 [8]

Place stitch marker in first st of rnd 1 and move it up after each round

Rnd 2: ch1, sc2, 3hdc-cl in each of next 4 sts, sc2, slst in beg ch1

Rnds 3–8: ch1, sc1 in each st, slst in beg ch1 (6 rnds)

Rnd 9: ch1, sc7, sc2 in last st, slst in beg ch1 [9]

Change to Yarn A

Rnd 10: ch1, sc4, sc3 in next st, sc4, slst in beg ch1 [11]

Rnd 11: ch1, sc5, sc3 in next st, sc5, slst in beg ch1 [13]

Rnd 12: ch1, sc6, sc3 in next st, sc6, slst in beg ch1 [15]

Rnds 13–14: ch1, sc1 in each st, slst in beg ch1

Rnd 15: ch1, sc4, sc2tog, sc3, sc2tog, sc4, slst in beg ch1 [13]

Fasten off.

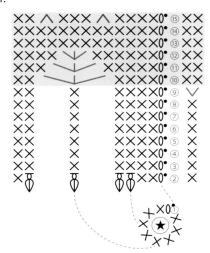

Back Legs (make 2)

With Yarn B, make a magic ring.

Rnd 1: ch1 (does not count as a st throughout), sc8 in magic ring, slst in beg ch1 [8]

Place stitch marker in first st of rnd 1 and move it up after each round

Rnd 2: ch1, sc2, 3hdc-cl in each of next 4 sts, sc2, slst in beg ch1

Rnds 3–8: ch1, sc1 in each st, slst in beg ch1 (6 rnds)

Rnd 9: ch1, sc7, sc2 in last st, slst in beg ch1 [9]

Change to Yarn A

Rnd 10: ch1, sc4, sc5 in next st, sc4, slst in beg ch1 [13]

Rnd 11: ch1, sc6, sc5 in next st, sc6, slst in beg ch1 [17]

Rnds 12–14: ch1, sc1 in each st, slst in beg ch1 (3 rnds)

Rnd 15: ch1, sc5, sc2tog, sc3, sc2tog, sc5, slst in beg ch1 [15]

Fasten off.

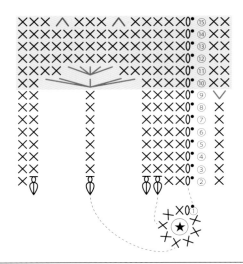

Ears (make 2)

With Yarn A, make a magic ring.

Rnd 1: ch1 (does not count as a st throughout), sc6 in magic ring, slst in beg ch1 [6]

Place stitch marker in first st of rnd 1 and move it up after each round

Rnd 2: ch1, sc2 in first st, sc4, sc2 in last st, slst in beg ch1 [8]

Rnd 3: in Yarn A, ch1, sc2 in first st, in Yarn B sc2, in Yarn A sc2, in Yarn B sc2, in Yarn A sc2 in next st, slst in beg ch1 [10]

Rnd 4: in Yarn A, ch1, sc2 in first st, in Yarn B sc3, in Yarn A sc2, in Yarn B sc3, in Yarn A sc2 in next st, slst in beg ch1 [12]

Rnd 5: in Yarn A, ch1, sc2 in first st, in Yarn B sc4, in Yarn A sc2, in Yarn B sc4, in Yarn A sc2 in next st, slst in beg ch1 [14]

Rnd 6: in Yarn A, ch1, sc2 in first st, in Yarn B sc5, in Yarn A sc2, in Yarn B sc5, in Yarn A sc2 in next st, slst in beg ch1 [16]

Rnd 7: in Yarn A, ch1, sc2 in first st, in Yarn B sc6, in Yarn A sc2, in Yarn B sc6, in Yarn A sc2 in next st, slst in beg ch1 [18]

Rnd 8: in Yarn A, ch1, sc2 in first st, in Yarn B sc7, in Yarn A sc2, in Yarn B sc7, in Yarn A sc2 in next st, slst in beg ch1 [20]

To make second ear, switch the colors, using Yarn B instead of Yarn A and vice versa.

Right ear:
Yarn B
Left ear:
Yarn A

Right ear:
Yarn A
Left ear:
Yarn B

Inside center

FINISHED SIZE

7" (18 cm) tall × 10¼" (26 cm) long

Location	Yarn Used	Yarn Length
Head	C, D	¾"–2½" (2–6 cm)
Body		1½"–3⅛" (4–8 cm)
Tail		3⅛" (8 cm)
Muzzle	C	⅜"–⅝" (1–1.5 cm)
Legs	C, D	1¼" (3 cm)
Ears		1½" (4 cm)

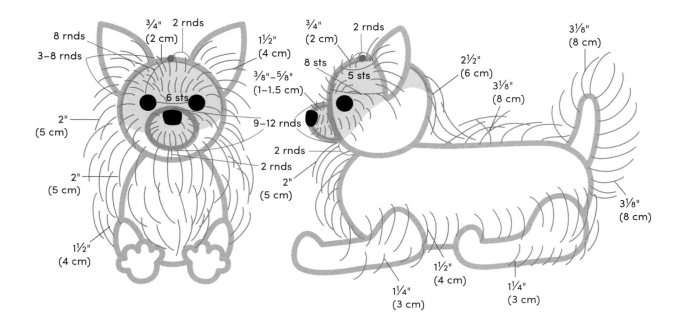

- For grafting, always use a total of 4 strands (2 of the sport weight acrylic and 2 of the light fingering weight acrylic/mohair blend).
- Brush the front and back with a slicker brush before grafting the ears.
- Mix Yarns C and D for the decorative fur in front of the ears. Attach this decorative fur to the bottom 3 rounds of the ears.
- When grafting the yarn to the face and chest, use the same yarn colors used to crochet the head and body (refer to the crochet diagrams on pages 78 and 77 for color placement).
- Graft yarn to the legs only in the areas where they attach to the body. Do not graft yarn to the paws.
- ▢ = Needle felt the areas shaded in light blue in order to compress the yarn and shape the head.
- Use Yarn C when grafting the top of the tail and Yarn D when grafting the bottom of the tail.

Long Haired Chihuahua / Sit

TOOLS & MATERIALS

- H/8 (5 mm) crochet hook
- 105 yards (80 g) bulky weight acrylic yarn in black
- 79 yds (60 g) bulky weight acrylic yarn in white
- 158 yds (40 g) sport weight acrylic yarn in black
- 79 yds (20 g) sport weight acrylic yarn in white
- 175 yds (40 g) of light fingering weight acrylic/mohair blend yarn in black
- 88 yards (20 g) of light fingering weight acrylic/mohair blend yarn in white

- Pair of 18 mm black plastic toy safety eyes
- One 21 mm black plastic toy safety nose
- Polyester fiber fill toy stuffing (about 40 g)
- Stitch marker
- Yarn needle
- Felting needle
- Slicker brush

YARN COMBINATION CHART

Use		Yarn Type	Yarn Color	Strands
Crocheting the Foundation	A	Bulky weight acrylic	Black	1 strand
	B	Bulky weight acrylic	White	1 strand
Grafting the Fur	C	Sport weight acrylic	Black	2 strands
		Light fingering weight acrylic/mohair blend	Black	2 strands
	D	Sport weight acrylic	White	2 strands
		Light fingering weight acrylic/mohair blend	White	2 strands

CONSTRUCTION STEPS

1. Crochet the body, head, front legs, back legs, ears, muzzle, and tail following instructions on pages 82–84 (also see pages 45–52).

2. Stuff and assemble the body parts following the instructions for the sit pose on pages 53–55.

3. Graft yarn according to the lengths listed on page 85 (refer to pages 56–58 for general grafting instructions).

4. Follow the techniques on page 58 to loosen the yarn and trim the fur into shape. Use the photos at right as a reference.

Front

Side

Back

CROCHET INSTRUCTIONS

Crochet Symbol Key

★ = magic ring

0 = ch st

• = slst

∧ = ⩕ = sc2tog

∨ = ⩔ = sc2 in next st

⩊ = 5 single crochet increase

⑂ = Cluster stitch variation with 3 half double crochet (refer to page 52)

Yarn Color Key

▨ = Yarn A

☐ = Yarn B

Body (make 1)

With Yarn B, make a magic ring.

Rnd 1: ch1 (does not count as a st throughout), sc6 in magic ring, slst in beg ch1 [6]

Place stitch marker in first st of rnd 1 and move it up after each round

Rnd 2: ch1, (sc2 in next st) 6 times, slst in beg ch1 [12]

Rnd 3: ch1, (sc1, sc2 in next st) 6 times, slst in beg ch1 [18]

Rnd 4: in Yarn A ch1, (sc2, sc2 in next st) twice, in Yarn B (sc2, sc2 in next st) twice, in Yarn A (sc2, sc2 in next st) twice, slst in beg ch1 [24]

Rnd 5: in Yarn A ch1, sc2 in next st, sc7, in Yarn B sc8, in Yarn A sc7, sc2 in next st, slst in beg ch1 [26]

Rnds 6–9: in Yarn A ch1, sc9, in Yarn B sc8, in Yarn A sc9, slst in beg ch1 (4 rnds)

Rnd 10: in Yarn A ch1, sc1, sc2tog, sc6, in Yarn B sc8, in Yarn A sc6, sc2tog, sc1, slst in beg ch1 [24]

Rnd 11: in Yarn A ch1, sc8, in Yarn B sc8, in Yarn A sc8, slst in beg ch1

Rnd 12: in Yarn A ch1, sc1, sc2tog, sc5, in Yarn B sc8, in Yarn A sc5, sc2tog, sc1, slst in beg ch1 [22]

Rnd 13: in Yarn A ch1, sc7, in Yarn B sc8, in Yarn A sc7, slst in beg ch1

Rnd 14: in Yarn A ch1, sc1, sc2tog, sc5, in Yarn B sc2 in next st, sc4, sc2 in next st, in Yarn A sc5, sc2tog, sc1, slst in beg ch1 [22]

Rnd 15: in Yarn A ch1, sc7, in Yarn B sc8, in Yarn A sc7, slst in beg ch1

Rnd 16: in Yarn A ch1, sc7, in Yarn B sc3, in Yarn A sc2, in Yarn B sc3, in Yarn A sc7, slst in beg ch1

Rnds 17–18: in Yarn A only, ch1, sc1 in each st to end, slst in beg ch1 (2 rnds)

Rnd 19: in Yarn A ch1, sc1, sc2tog, sc5, sc2 in next st, in Yarn B sc4, in Yarn A sc2 in next st, sc5, sc2tog, sc1, slst in beg ch1 [22]

Rnds 20–22: in Yarn A ch1, sc7, in Yarn B sc8, in Yarn A sc7, slst in beg ch1 (3 rnds)

Rnd 23: in Yarn A ch1, sc1, sc2tog, sc4, in Yarn B sc2tog, sc4, sc2tog, in Yarn A sc4, sc2tog, sc1, slst in beg ch1 [18]

Fasten off.

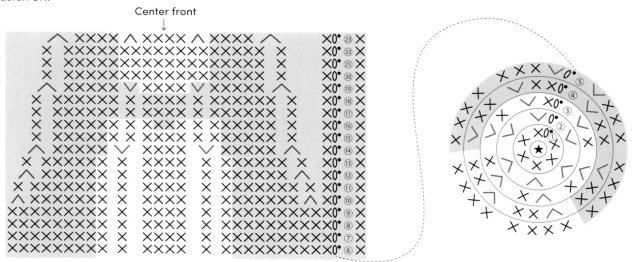

Center front

Head (make 1)

With Yarn A, make a magic ring.

Rnd 1: ch1 (does not count as a st throughout), sc6 in magic ring, slst in beg ch1 [6]

Place stitch marker in first st of rnd 1 and move it up after each round

Rnd 2: ch1, (sc2 in next st) 6 times, slst in beg ch1 [12]

Rnd 3: ch1, (sc1, sc2 in next st) 6 times, slst in beg ch1 [18]

Rnd 4: ch1, (sc2, sc2 in next st) 6 times, slst in beg ch1 [24]

Rnd 5: ch1, (sc3, sc2 in next st) 6 times, slst in beg ch1 [30]

Rnd 6: in Yarn A ch1, sc14, in Yarn B sc1, in Yarn A sc15, slst in beg ch1

Rnds 7–9: in Yarn A ch1, sc14, in Yarn B sc2, in Yarn A sc14, slst in beg ch1 (3 rnds)

Rnd 10: in Yarn A ch1, sc13, in Yarn B sc4, in Yarn A sc13, slst in beg ch1

Rnd 11: in Yarn A ch1, sc2, sc2tog, sc3, sc2tog, sc2, sc2tog, in Yarn B sc4, in Yarn A sc2tog, sc2, sc2tog, sc3, sc2tog, sc2, slst in beg ch1 [24]

Rnd 12: in Yarn A ch1, sc8, sc2tog, in Yarn B sc4, in Yarn A sc2tog, sc8, slst in beg ch1 [22]

Rnd 13: In Yarn A only, ch1, sc4, (sc2tog, sc2) 3 times, sc2tog, sc4, slst in beg ch1 [18]

Rnd 14: In Yarn A only, ch1, sc1 in each st to end, slst in beg ch1
Fasten off.

Attach toy safety eyes to front of face at position shown in diagram on page 85, between rnds 8 and 9, leaving 6 sts between eyes.

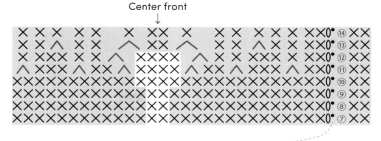

Center front

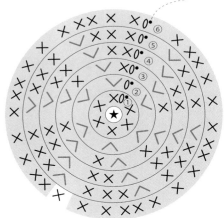

Muzzle (make 1)

With Yarn B, make 5ch.

Rnd 1: skip first ch, sc1 in next ch, sc1 in next 2 ch, sc3 in last ch, rotate and work along opposite side of chain, sc1 in next 2 ch, sc2 in last ch, slst in skipped ch at beg of rnd [10]

Place stitch marker in first st of rnd 1 and move it up after each round

Rnd 2: ch1, (sc4, sc2 in next st) twice, slst in beg ch1 [12]

Rnd 3: ch1, sc1 in each st, slst in beg ch1
Fasten off.

Add toy safety nose at position shown in diagram, at center front of muzzle, between rnds 1 and 2.

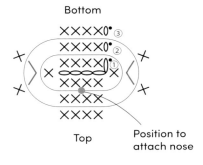

Bottom

Top

Position to attach nose

Tail (make 1)

With Yarn A, make a magic ring.

Rnd 1: ch1 (does not count as a st throughout), sc5 in magic ring, slst in beg ch1 [5]

Place stitch marker in first st of rnd 1 and move it up after each round

Rnd 2: ch1, sc4, sc2 in last st, slst in beg ch1 [6]

Rnds 3–7: ch1, sc1 in each st, slst in beg ch1 (5 rnds)
Fasten off.

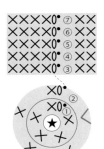

Front Legs (make 2)

With Yarn B, make a magic ring.

Rnd 1: ch1 (does not count as a st throughout), sc8 in magic ring, slst in beg ch1 [8]

Place stitch marker in first st of rnd 1 and move it up after each round

Rnd 2: ch1, sc2, 3hdc-cl in each of next 4 sts, sc2, slst in beg ch1

Rnds 3–8: ch1, sc1 in each st, slst in beg ch1 (6 rnds)

Change to Yarn A

Rnd 9: ch1, sc7, sc2 in next st, slst in beg ch1 [9]

Rnd 10: ch1, sc1 in each st to end, slst in beg ch1

Rnd 11: ch1, sc8, sc2 in next st, slst in beg ch1 [10]

Rnd 12: ch1, sc9, sc2 in next st, slst in beg ch1 [11]

Rnd 13: ch1, sc10, sc2 in next st, slst in beg ch1 [12]

Fasten off.

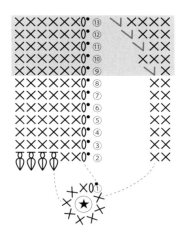

Back Legs (make 2)

With Yarn B, make a magic ring.

Rnd 1: ch1 (does not count as a st throughout), sc8 in magic ring, slst in beg ch1 [8]

Place stitch marker in first st of rnd 1 and move it up after each round

Rnd 2: ch1, sc2, 3hdc-cl in each of next 4 sts, sc2, slst in beg ch1

Rnds 3–8: ch1, sc1 in each st, slst in beg ch1 (6 rnds)

Rnd 9: ch1, sc7, sc2 in next st, slst in beg ch1 [9]

Change to Yarn A

Rnd 10: ch1, sc4, sc5 in next st, sc4, slst in beg ch1 [13]

Rnd 11: ch1, sc6, sc5 in next st, sc6, slst in beg ch1 [17]

Rnds 12–14: ch1, sc1 in each st, slst in beg ch1 (3 rnds)

Rnd 15: ch1, sc5, sc2tog, sc3, sc2tog, sc5, slst in beg ch1 [15]

Fasten off.

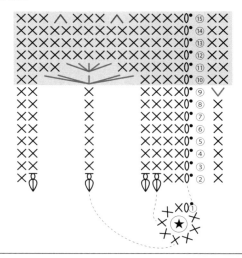

Ears (make 2)

With Yarn A, make a magic ring.

Rnd 1: ch1 (does not count as a st throughout), sc6 in magic ring, slst in beg ch1 [6]

Place stitch marker in first st of rnd 1 and move it up after each round

Rnd 2: ch1, sc2 in first st, sc4, sc2 in last st, slst in beg ch1 [8]

Rnd 3: in Yarn A, ch1, sc2 in first st, in Yarn B sc2, in Yarn A sc2, in Yarn B sc2, in Yarn A sc2 in next st, slst in beg ch1 [10]

Rnd 4: in Yarn A, ch1, sc2 in first st, in Yarn B sc3, in Yarn A sc2, in Yarn B sc3, in Yarn A sc2 in next st, slst in beg ch1 [12]

Rnd 5: in Yarn A, ch1, sc2 in first st, in Yarn B sc4, in Yarn A sc2, in Yarn B sc4, in Yarn A sc2 in next st, slst in beg ch1 [14]

Rnd 6: in Yarn A, ch1, sc2 in first st, in Yarn B sc5, in Yarn A sc2, in Yarn B sc5, in Yarn A sc2 in next st, slst in beg ch1 [16]

Rnd 7: in Yarn A, ch1, sc2 in first st, in Yarn B sc6, in Yarn A sc2, in Yarn B sc6, in Yarn A sc2 in next st, slst in beg ch1 [18]

Rnd 8: in Yarn A, ch1, sc2 in first st, in Yarn B sc7, in Yarn A sc2, in Yarn B sc7, in Yarn A sc2 in next st, slst in beg ch1 [20]

To make second ear, switch the colors, using Yarn B instead of Yarn A and vice versa.

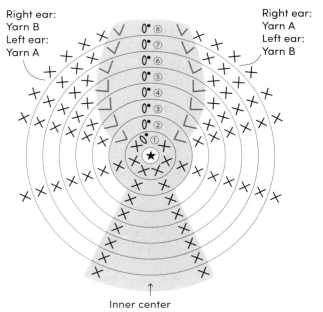

Right ear:
Yarn B
Left ear:
Yarn A

Right ear:
Yarn A
Left ear:
Yarn B

↑
Inner center

GRAFTING & FINISHING

Location	Yarn Used	Yarn Length
Head	C, D	³⁄₄"–2½" (2–6 cm)
Body	C, D	1½"–3⅛" (4–8 cm)
Tail	C, D	3⅛" (8 cm)
Muzzle	D	⅜"–⅝" (1–1.5 cm)
Legs	C, D	1¼"–1½" (3–4 cm)
Ears	C, D	1½" (4 cm)

FINISHED SIZE

9½" (24 cm) tall × 7" (18 cm) long

Eyebrow Placement

Refer to page 59 for more detailed instructions on making the eyebrows.

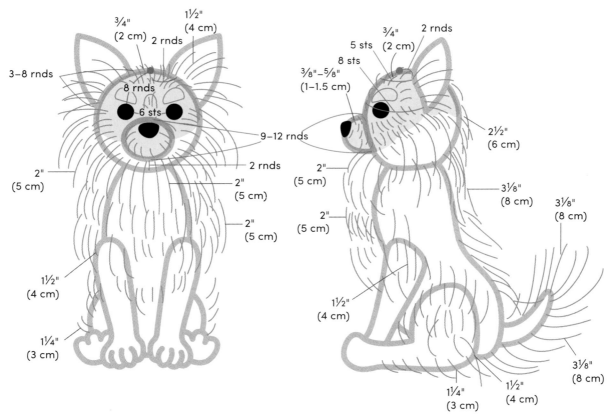

- For grafting, always use a total of 4 strands (2 of the sport weight acrylic and 2 of the light fingering weight acrylic/mohair blend).
- Brush the front and back with a slicker brush before grafting the ears.
- Mix Yarns C and D for the decorative fur in front of the ears. Attach this decorative fur to the bottom 3 rounds of the ears.
- When grafting the yarn to the face and chest, use the same yarn colors used to crochet the head and body (refer to the crochet diagrams on pages 83 and 82 for color placement).

- Graft yarn to the legs only in the areas where they attach to the body. Do not graft yarn to the paws.
- ░ = Needle felt the areas shaded in light blue in order to compress the yarn and shape the head.
- Refer to page 59 for instructions on embroidering and needle felting the eyebrows.
- Use Yarn C when grafting the top of the tail and Yarn D when grafting the bottom of the tail.

𝒫omeranian / Sit

TOOLS & MATERIALS

- P/15 (10 mm) crochet hook
- N/13 (9 mm) crochet hook
- K/10½ (7 mm) crochet hook
- 303 yds (230 g) bulky weight acrylic yarn in dark beige
- 473 yds (120 g) sport weight acrylic yarn in golden brown
- 478 yds (110 g) of light fingering weight acrylic/mohair blend yarn in brown

- Pair of 15 mm black plastic toy safety eyes
- One 21 mm black plastic toy safety nose
- Polyester fiber fill toy stuffing (about 50 g)
- Stitch marker
- Yarn needle
- Felting needle
- Slicker brush

YARN COMBINATION CHART

Use		Yarn Type	Yarn Color	Amount	Strands	Crochet Hook Size
Crocheting the Foundation	A	Bulky weight acrylic	Dark beige	237 yds (180 g)	2 strands	P/15 (10 mm)
	B	Bulky weight acrylic	Dark beige	66 yds (50 g)	1 strand	N/13 (9 mm)
		Sport weight acrylic	Golden brown	79 yds (20 g)	1 strand	
		Light fingering weight acrylic/mohair blend	Brown	88 yds (20 g)	1 strand	
Crocheting the Foundation/ Grafting the Fur	C	Sport weight acrylic	Golden brown	394 yds (100 g)	2 strands	K/10½ (7 mm) (for the foundation only)
			Brown	394 yds (90 g)	2 strands	

CONSTRUCTION STEPS

1. Crochet the body, head, front legs, back legs, ears, muzzle, and tail following instructions on pages 87–89 (also see pages 45–52).

2. Stuff and assemble the body parts following the instructions for the sit pose on pages 53–55.

3. Graft yarn according to the lengths listed on page 90 (refer to pages 56–58 for general grafting instructions).

4. Follow the techniques on page 58 to loosen the yarn and trim the fur into shape. Use the photos at right as a reference.

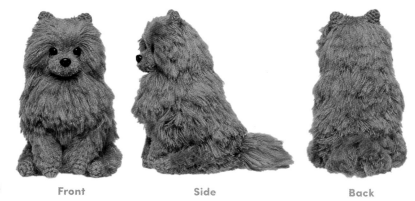

Front   Side   Back

CROCHET INSTRUCTIONS

Crochet Symbol Key

★ = magic ring ∧ = ⋀ = sc2tog ⋁ = 3 single crochet increase

0 = ch st ⋁ = ⋎ = sc2 in next st ⋓ = 5 single crochet increase

• = slst

Body (make 1)

With Yarn A and P/15 (10 mm) hook, make a magic ring.

Rnd 1: ch1 (does not count as a st throughout), sc6 in magic ring, slst in beg ch1 [6]

Place stitch marker in first st of rnd 1 and move it up after each round

Rnd 2: ch1, (sc2 in next st) 6 times, slst in beg ch1 [12]

Rnd 3: ch1, (sc1, sc2 in next st) 6 times, slst in beg ch1 [18]

Rnd 4: ch1, (sc2, sc2 in next st) 6 times, slst in beg ch1 [24]

Rnd 5: ch1, sc2 in next st, sc22, sc2 in next st, slst in beg ch1 [26]

Rnds 6–9: ch1, sc1 in each st, slst in beg ch1 (4 rnds)

Rnd 10: ch1, sc1, sc2tog, sc20, sc2tog, sc1, slst in beg ch1 [24]

Rnd 11: ch1, sc1 in each st, slst in beg ch1

Rnd 12: ch1, sc1, sc2tog, sc18, sc2tog, sc1, slst in beg ch1 [22]

Rnd 13: ch1, sc1 in each st, slst in beg ch1

Rnd 14: ch1, sc1, sc2tog, sc5, sc2 in next st, sc4, sc2 in next st, sc5, sc2tog, sc1, slst in beg ch1 [22]

Rnds 15–18: ch1, sc1 in each st, slst in beg ch1 (4 rnds)

Rnd 19: ch1, sc1, sc2tog, sc5, sc2 in next st, sc4, sc2 in next st, sc5, sc2tog, sc1, slst in beg ch1 [22]

Rnds 20–22: ch1, sc1 in each st, slst in beg ch1 (3 rnds)

Rnd 23: ch1, sc1, (sc2tog, sc4) 3 times, sc2tog, sc1, slst in beg ch1 [18]

Fasten off.

Center front

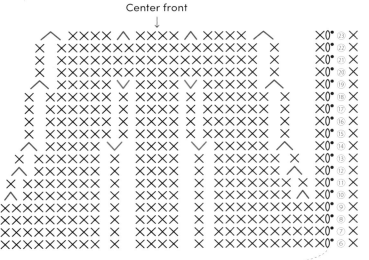

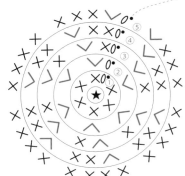

Head (make 1)

With Yarn A and P/15 (10 mm) hook, make a magic ring.

Rnd 1: ch1 (does not count as a st throughout), sc6 in magic ring, slst in beg ch1 [6]

Place stitch marker in first st of rnd 1 and move it up after each round

Rnd 2: ch1, (sc2 in next st) 6 times, slst in beg ch1 [12]

Rnd 3: ch1, (sc1, sc2 in next st) 6 times, slst in beg ch1 [18]

Rnd 4: ch1, (sc2, sc2 in next st) 6 times, slst in beg ch1 [24]

Rnds 5–9: ch1, sc1 in each st, slst in beg ch1 (5 rnds)

Rnd 10: ch1, sc8, sc2tog, sc4, sc2tog, sc8, slst in beg ch1 [22]

Rnd 11: ch1, sc4, (sc2tog, sc2) 3 times, sc2tog, sc4, slst in beg ch1 [18]

Rnd 12: ch1, sc1 in each st to end, slst in beg ch1

Fasten off.

Attach toy safety eyes to front of face at position shown in diagram on page 90, between rnds 6 and 7, leaving 5 sts between eyes.

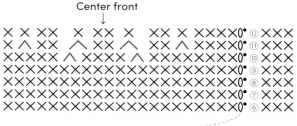

Center front

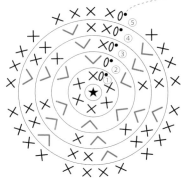

Front Legs (make 2)

With Yarn B and N/13 (9mm) hook, make a magic ring.

Rnd 1: ch1 (does not count as a st throughout), sc8 in magic ring, slst in beg ch1 [8]

Place stitch marker in first st of rnd 1 and move it up after each round

Rnds 2–5: ch1, sc1 in each st, slst in beg ch1 (4 rnds)

Rnd 6: ch1, sc7, sc2 in next st, slst in beg ch1 [9]

Rnd 7: ch1, sc1 in each st to end, slst in beg ch1

Rnd 8: ch1, sc8, sc2 in next st, slst in beg ch1 [10]

Rnd 9: ch1, sc1 in each st to end, slst in beg ch1

Rnd 10: ch1, sc9, sc2 in next st, slst in beg ch1 [11]

Rnd 11: ch1, sc1 in each st to end, slst in beg ch1

Rnd 12: ch1, sc10, sc2 in next st, slst in beg ch1 [12]

Rnd 13: ch1, sc1 in each st to end, slst in beg ch1

Fasten off.

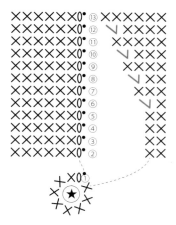

Back Legs (make 2)

With Yarn B and N/13 (9 mm) hook, make a magic ring.

Rnd 1: ch1 (does not count as a st throughout), sc8 in magic ring, slst in beg ch1 [8]

Place stitch marker in first st of rnd 1 and move it up after each round

Rnds 2–6: ch1, sc1 in each st, slst in beg ch1 (5 rnds)

Rnd 7: ch1, sc7, sc2 in next st, slst in beg ch1 [9]

Rnd 8: ch1, sc4, sc5 in next st, sc4, slst in beg ch1 [13]

Rnd 9: ch1, sc6, sc5 in next st, sc6, slst in beg ch1 [17]

Rnd 10: ch1, sc8, sc3 in next st, sc8, slst in beg ch1 [19]

Rnds 11–13: ch1, sc1 in each st, slst in beg ch1 (3 rnds)

Rnd 14: ch1, sc6, sc2tog, sc3, sc2tog, sc6, slst in beg ch1 [17]

Fasten off.

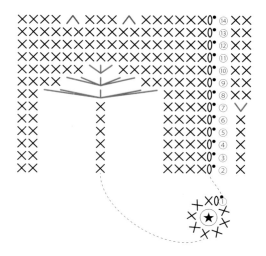

Ears (make 2)

With Yarn C and K/10½ (7 mm) hook, make a magic ring.

Rnd 1: ch1 (does not count as a st throughout), sc5 in magic ring, slst in beg ch1 [5]

Place stitch marker in first st of rnd 1 and move it up after each round

Rnd 2: ch1, sc2 in first st, sc3, sc2 in last st, slst in beg ch1 [7]
Rnd 3: ch1, sc2 in first st, sc5, sc2 in last st, slst in beg ch1 [9]
Rnd 4: ch1, sc2 in first st, sc7, sc2 in last st, slst in beg ch1 [11]
Rnd 5: ch1, sc2 in first st, sc9, sc2 in last st, slst in beg ch1 [13]
Rnd 6: ch1, sc2 in first st, sc11, sc2 in last st, slst in beg ch1 [15]
Rnd 7: ch1, sc2 in first st, sc13, sc2 in last st, slst in beg ch1 [17]
Fasten off.

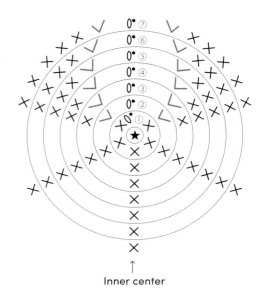

Inner center

Muzzle (make 1)

With Yarn B and N/13 (9 mm) hook, make 4ch.

Rnd 1: skip first ch, sc1 in next ch, sc1 in next ch, sc3 in last ch, rotate and work along opposite side of chain, sc1 in next ch, sc2 in last ch, slst in skipped ch at beg of rnd [8]

Place stitch marker in first st of rnd 1 and move it up after each round

Rnd 2: ch1, (sc3, sc2 in next st) twice, slst in beg ch1 [10]
Rnd 3: ch1, sc3, sc2 in next st, sc5, sc2 in next st, slst in beg ch1 [12]
Fasten off.

Add toy safety nose at position shown in diagram, at center front of muzzle, between rnds 1 and 2.

Bottom

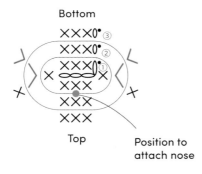

Top

Position to attach nose

Tail (make 1)

With Yarn A and P/15 (10 mm) hook, make a magic ring.

Rnd 1: ch1 (does not count as a st throughout), sc5 in magic ring, slst in beg ch1 [5]

Place stitch marker in first st of rnd 1 and move it up after each round

Rnd 2: ch1, sc4, sc2 in last st, slst in beg ch1 [6]
Rnds 3–7: ch1, sc1 in each st, slst in beg ch1 (5 rnds)
Fasten off.

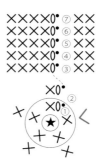

GRAFTING & FINISHING

Location	Yarn Used	Yarn Length
Head		1¼"–1½" (3–4 cm)
Body		2½"–3½" (6–9 cm)
Tail	C	3⅛"–4" (8–10 cm)
Muzzle		⅜" (1 cm)
Legs		¾"–1½" (2–4 cm)
Ears		No grafting

FINISHED SIZE

11¾" (30 cm) tall × 9½" (24 cm) long

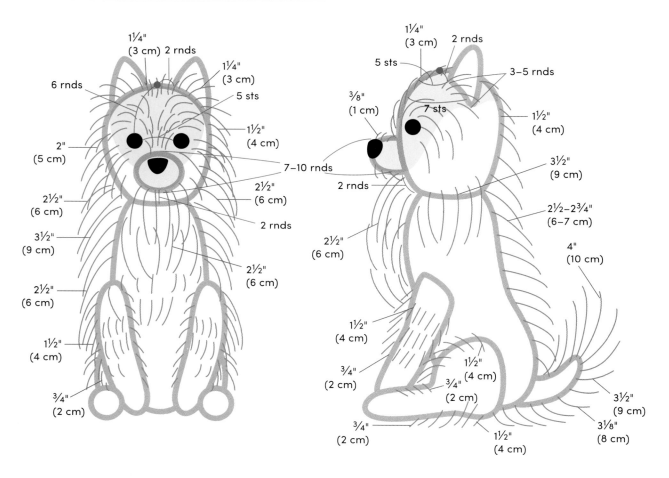

- For grafting, always use a total of 4 strands (2 of the sport weight acrylic and 2 of the light fingering weight acrylic/mohair blend).
- Brush the front and back with a slicker brush before grafting the ears.
- Use a felting needle to arrange the flow of the fur as shown on page 59.
- ▢ = Needle felt the areas shaded in light blue in order to compress the yarn and shape the head.
- Needle felt the grafted yarn so that it becomes thinner toward the tip of the leg.

TOOLS & MATERIALS

- P/15 (10 mm) crochet hook
- N/13 (9 mm) crochet hook
- K/10½ (7 mm) crochet hook
- 263 yds (200 g) bulky weight acrylic yarn in black
- 66 yds (50 g) bulky weight acrylic yarn in dark beige
- 158 yds (40 g) sport weight acrylic yarn in golden brown
- 276 yds (70 g) sport weight acrylic yarn in black
- 176 yds (40 g) of light fingering weight acrylic/mohair blend yarn in brown

- 307 yds (70 g) of light fingering weight acrylic/mohair blend yarn in black
- Pair of 15 mm black plastic toy safety eyes
- One 21 mm black plastic toy safety nose
- Polyester fiber fill toy stuffing (about 50 g)
- Stitch marker
- Yarn needle
- Felting needle
- Slicker brush

YARN COMBINATION CHART

Use		Yarn Type	Yarn Color	Amount	Strands	Crochet Hook Size
Crocheting the Foundation	A	Bulky weight acrylic	Black	263 yds (200 g)	2 strands	P/15 (10 mm)
	B	Bulky weight acrylic	Dark beige	66 yds (50 g)	1 strand	N/13 (9 mm)
		Sport weight acrylic	Golden brown	79 yds (20 g)	1 strand	
		Light fingering weight acrylic/mohair blend	Brown	88 yds (20 g)	1 strand	
Crocheting the Foundation/ Grafting the Fur	C	Sport weight acrylic	Black	276 yds (70 g)	2 strands	K/10½ (7 mm) (for the foundation only)
		Light fingering weight acrylic/mohair blend	Black	307 yds (70 g)	2 strands	
Grafting the Fur	D	Sport weight acrylic	Golden brown	79 yds (20 g)	2 strands	
		Light fingering weight acrylic/mohair blend	Brown	88 yds (20 g)	2 strands	

CONSTRUCTION STEPS

1. Crochet the body, head, front legs, back legs, ears, muzzle, and tail following instructions on pages 92–94 (also see pages 45–52).

2. Stuff and assemble the body parts following the instructions for the stand pose on pages 54–55.

3. Graft yarn according to the lengths listed on page 95 (refer to pages 56–58 for general grafting instructions).

4. Follow the techniques on page 58 to loosen the yarn and trim the fur into shape. Use the photos at right as a reference.

Front   Side   Back

Crochet Symbol Key

★ = magic ring ∧ = ⋀ = sc2tog

0 = ch st ∨ = ⩔ = sc2 in next st

• = slst

Body (make 1)

With Yarn A and P/15 (10 mm) hook, make a magic ring.

Rnd 1: ch1 (does not count as a st throughout), sc6 in magic ring, slst in beg ch1 [6]

Place stitch marker in first st of rnd 1 and move it up after each round.

Rnd 2: ch1, (sc2 in next st) 6 times, slst in beg ch1 [12]

Rnd 3: ch1, (sc1, sc2 in next st) 6 times, slst in beg ch1 [18]

Rnd 4: ch1, (sc2, sc2 in next st) 6 times, slst in beg ch1 [24]

Rnds 5–24: ch1, sc1 in each st, slst in beg ch1 (20 rnds)

Rnd 25: ch1, (sc2, sc2tog) 6 times, slst in beg ch1 [18]

Begin to stuff body firmly.

Rnd 26: ch1, (sc1, sc2tog) 6 times, slst in beg ch1 [12]

Rnd 27: ch1, (sc2tog) 6 times, slst in beg ch1 [6]

Fasten off leaving a long tail end. Add more stuffing if needed then thread yarn through stitches of last round and pull tightly to close.

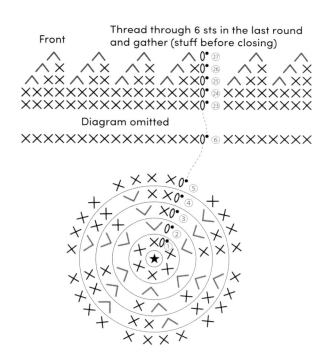

Front

Thread through 6 sts in the last round and gather (stuff before closing)

Diagram omitted

Head (make 1)

With Yarn A and P/15 (10 mm) hook, make a magic ring.
Rnd 1: ch1 (does not count as a st throughout), sc6 in magic ring, slst in beg ch1 [6]
Place stitch marker in first st of rnd 1 and move it up after each round
Rnd 2: ch1, (sc2 in next st) 6 times, slst in beg ch1 [12]
Rnd 3: ch1, (sc1, sc2 in next st) 6 times, slst in beg ch1 [18]
Rnd 4: ch1, (sc2, sc2 in next st) 6 times, slst in beg ch1 [24]
Rnds 5–9: ch1, sc1 in each st, slst in beg ch1 (5 rnds)
Rnd 10: ch1, sc8, sc2tog, sc4, sc2tog, sc8, slst in beg ch1 [22]
Rnd 11: ch1, sc4, (sc2tog, sc2) 3 times, sc2tog, sc4, slst in beg ch1 [18]
Rnd 12: ch1, sc1 in each st, slst in beg ch1
Fasten off.
Attach toy safety eyes to front of face at position shown in diagram on page 95, between rnds 6 and 7, leaving 5 sts between eyes.

Center front

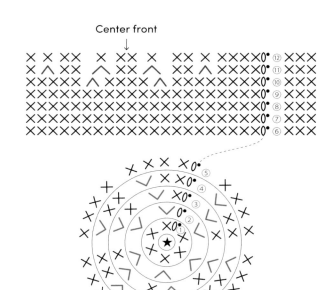

Front Legs (make 2)

With Yarn B and N/13 (9mm) hook, make a magic ring.
Rnd 1: ch1 (does not count as a st throughout), sc8 in magic ring, slst in beg ch1 [8]
Place stitch marker in first st of rnd 1 and move it up after each round
Rnds 2–5: ch1, sc1 in each st, slst in beg ch1 (4 rnds)
Rnd 6: ch1, sc7, sc2 in next st, slst in beg ch1 [9]
Rnd 7: ch1, sc1 in each st to end, slst in beg ch1
Rnd 8: ch1, sc8, sc2 in next st, slst in beg ch1 [10]
Rnd 9: ch1, sc1 in each st to end, slst in beg ch1
Rnd 10: ch1, sc9, sc2 in next st, slst in beg ch1 [11]
Rnd 11: ch1, sc1 in each st to end, slst in beg ch1
Rnd 12: ch1, sc10, sc2 in next st, slst in beg ch1 [12]
Rnd 13: ch1, sc1 in each st to end, slst in beg ch1
Fasten off.

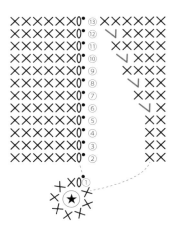

Back Legs (make 2)

With Yarn B and N/13 (9 mm) hook, make a magic ring.
Rnd 1: ch1 (does not count as a st throughout), sc8 in magic ring, slst in beg ch1 [8]
Place stitch marker in first st of rnd 1 and move it up after each round
Rnds 2–6: ch1, sc1 in each st, slst in beg ch1 (5 rnds)
Rnd 7: ch1, sc7, sc2 in next st, slst in beg ch1 [9]
Rnd 8: ch1, sc8, sc2 in next st, slst in beg ch1 [10]
Rnd 9: ch1, sc9, sc2 in next st, slst in beg ch1 [11]
Rnd 10: ch1, sc10, sc2 in next st, slst in beg ch1 [12]
Rnd 11: ch1, sc11, sc2 in next st, slst in beg ch1 [13]
Rnd 14: ch1, sc12, sc2 in next st, slst in beg ch1 [14]
Fasten off.

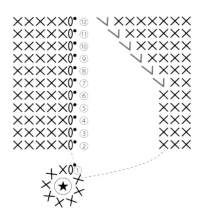

Ears (make 2)

With Yarn C and K/10½ (7 mm) hook, make a magic ring.
Rnd 1: ch1 (does not count as a st throughout), sc5 in magic ring, slst in beg ch1 [5]
Place stitch marker in first st of rnd 1 and move it up after each round
Rnd 2: ch1, sc2 in first st, sc3, sc2 in last st, slst in beg ch1 [7]
Rnd 3: ch1, sc2 in first st, sc5, sc2 in last st, slst in beg ch1 [9]
Rnd 4: ch1, sc2 in first st, sc7, sc2 in last st, slst in beg ch1 [11]
Rnd 5: ch1, sc2 in first st, sc9, sc2 in last st, slst in beg ch1 [13]
Rnd 6: ch1, sc2 in first st, sc11, sc2 in last st, slst in beg ch1 [15]
Rnd 7: ch1, sc2 in first st, sc13, sc2 in last st, slst in beg ch1 [17]
Fasten off.

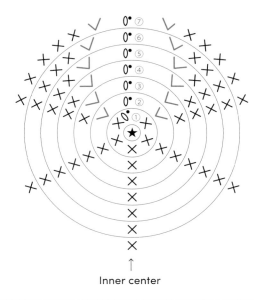

Inner center

Muzzle (make 1)

With Yarn B and N/13 (9 mm) hook, make 4ch.
Rnd 1: skip first ch, sc1 in next ch, sc1 in next ch, sc3 in last ch, rotate and work along opposite side of chain, sc1 in next ch, sc2 in last ch, slst in skipped ch at beg of rnd [8]
Place stitch marker in first st of rnd 1 and move it up after each round
Rnd 2: ch1, (sc3, sc2 in next st) twice, slst in beg ch1 [10]
Rnd 3: ch1, sc3, sc2 in next st, sc5, sc2 in next st, slst in beg ch1 [12]
Fasten off.
Add toy safety nose at position shown in diagram, at center front of muzzle, between rnds 1 and 2.

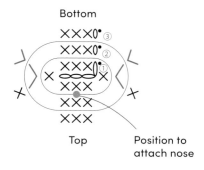

Bottom

Top

Position to attach nose

Tail (make 1)

With Yarn A and P/15 (10 mm) hook, make a magic ring.
Rnd 1: ch1 (does not count as a st throughout), sc5 in magic ring, slst in beg ch1 [5]
Place stitch marker in first st of rnd 1 and move it up after each round
Rnd 2: ch1, sc4, sc2 in last st, slst in beg ch1 [6]
Rnds 3–7: ch1, sc1 in each st, slst in beg ch1 (5 rnds)
Fasten off.

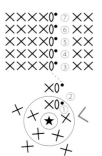

Location	Yarn Used	Yarn Length
Head		1¼"–2½" (3–6 cm)
Body	C, D	2½"–3½" (6–9 cm)
Tail		3⅛"–4" (8–10 cm)
Muzzle	D	⅜" (1 cm)
Legs	C, D	¾"–1½" (2–4 cm)
Ears		No grafting

FINISHED SIZE

10½" (27 cm) tall × 11¾" (30 cm) long

Eyebrow Placement

Refer to page 59 for more detailed instructions on making the eyebrows.

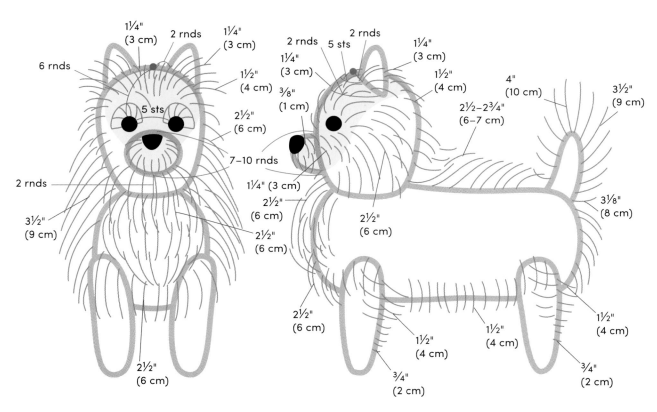

- For grafting, always use a total of 4 strands (2 of the sport weight acrylic and 2 of the light fingering weight acrylic/mohair blend).
- Graft the chest fur and the back side of the base of the legs with Yarn D.
- Refer to page 59 for instructions on embroidering and needle felting the eyebrows.
- ▢ = Needle felt the areas shaded in light blue in order to compress the yarn and shape the head.
- Use Yarn C when grafting the top of the tail and Yarn D when grafting the bottom of the tail.

𝒟achshund / Lie Down

Shown on page 23

TOOLS & MATERIALS

- P/15 (10 mm) crochet hook
- 329 yds (250 g) bulky weight acrylic yarn in beige
- 394 yds (100 g) sport weight acrylic yarn in light beige
- 394 yds (90 g) of light fingering weight acrylic/mohair blend yarn in cream

- Pair of 15 mm black plastic toy safety eyes
- One 20 mm black plastic toy safety nose
- Polyester fiber fill toy stuffing (about 60 g)
- Stitch marker
- Yarn needle
- Felting needle
- Slicker brush

YARN COMBINATION CHART

Area	Yarn Used		Yarn Color	Strands
Crocheting the Foundation	A	Bulky weight acrylic	Beige	2 strands
Grafting the Fur	B	Sport weight acrylic	Light beige	2 strands
		Light fingering weight acrylic/mohair blend	Cream	2 strands

CONSTRUCTION STEPS

1. Crochet the body, head, front legs, back legs, muzzle, and tail following instructions on pages 97–98 (also see pages 45–52). Make the ears as shown on page 60.

2. Stuff and assemble the body parts following the instructions for the lie down pose on pages 54–55.

3. Graft yarn according to the lengths listed on page 99 (refer to pages 56–58 for general grafting instructions).

4. Follow the techniques on page 58 to loosen the yarn and trim the fur into shape. Use the photos below as a reference.

Front   Side   Back

CROCHET INSTRUCTIONS

Crochet Symbol Key

★ = magic ring ∧ = ⩕ = sc2tog ⋁ = 3 single crochet increase

0 = ch st ⋁ = ⋓ = sc2 in next st

• = slst

Body (make 1)

With Yarn A, make a magic ring.

Rnd 1: ch1 (does not count as a st throughout), sc6 in magic ring, slst in beg ch1 [6]

Place stitch marker in first st of rnd 1 and move it up after each round.

Rnd 2: ch1, (sc2 in next st) 6 times, slst in beg ch1 [12]

Rnd 3: ch1, (sc1, sc2 in next st) 6 times, slst in beg ch1 [18]

Rnd 4: ch1, (sc2, sc2 in next st) 6 times, slst in beg ch1 [24]

Rnds 5–30: ch1, sc1 in each st, slst in beg ch1 (26 rnds)

Rnd 31: ch1, (sc2, sc2tog) 6 times, slst in beg ch1 [18]

Begin to stuff body firmly.

Rnd 32: ch1, (sc1, sc2tog) 6 times, slst in beg ch1 [12]

Rnd 33: ch1, (sc2tog) 6 times, slst in beg ch1 [6]

Fasten off leaving a long tail end. Add more stuffing if needed then thread yarn through stitches of last round and pull tightly to close.

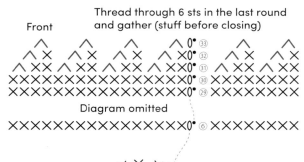

Front

Thread through 6 sts in the last round and gather (stuff before closing)

Diagram omitted

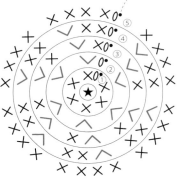

Head (make 1)

With Yarn A, make a magic ring.

Rnd 1: ch1 (does not count as a st throughout), sc6 in magic ring, slst in beg ch1 [6]

Place stitch marker in first st of rnd 1 and move it up after each round

Rnd 2: ch1, (sc2 in next st) 6 times, slst in beg ch1 [12]

Rnd 3: ch1, (sc1, sc2 in next st) 6 times, slst in beg ch1 [18]

Rnd 4: ch1, (sc2, sc2 in next st) 6 times, slst in beg ch1 [24]

Rnds 5–9: ch1, sc1 in each st, slst in beg ch1 (5 rnds)

Rnd 10: ch1, sc8, sc2tog, sc4, sc2tog, sc8, slst in beg ch1 [22]

Rnd 11: ch1, sc4, (sc2tog, sc2) 3 times, sc2tog, sc4, slst in beg ch1 [18]

Rnd 12: ch1, sc1, sc2 in next st, sc14, sc2 in next st, sc1, slst in beg ch1 [20]

Fasten off.

Attach toy safety eyes to front of face at position shown in diagram on page 99, between rnds 6 and 7, leaving 6 sts between eyes.

Center front

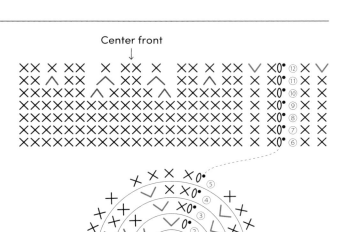

Front Legs (make 2)

With Yarn A, make a magic ring.

Rnd 1: ch1 (does not count as a st throughout), sc8 in magic ring, slst in beg ch1 [8]

Place stitch marker in first st of rnd 1 and move it up after each round

Rnd 2: ch1, sc1 in each st, slst in beg ch1

Rnd 3: ch1, sc2, (sc2tog) twice, sc2, slst in beg ch1 [6]

Rnds 4–5: ch1, sc1 in each st, slst in beg ch1 (2 rnds)

Rnd 6: ch1, sc5, sc2 in next st, slst in beg ch1 [7]

Rnd 7: ch1, sc6, sc2 in next st, slst in beg ch1 [8]

Rnd 8: ch1, sc7, sc2 in next st, slst in beg ch1 [9]

Rnd 9: ch1, sc8, sc2 in next st, slst in beg ch1 [10]

Fasten off.

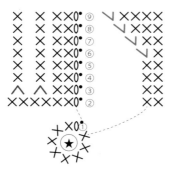

Back Legs (make 2)

With Yarn A, make a magic ring.

Rnd 1: ch1 (does not count as a st throughout), sc8 in magic ring, slst in beg ch1 [8]

Place stitch marker in first st of rnd 1 and move it up after each round

Rnd 2: ch1, sc1 in each st, slst in beg ch1

Rnd 3: ch1, sc2, (sc2tog) twice, sc2, slst in beg ch1 [6]

Rnd 4: ch1, sc1 in each st, slst in beg ch1

Rnd 5: ch1, sc5, sc2 in next st, slst in beg ch1 [7]

Rnd 6: ch1, sc3, sc3 in next st, sc3, slst in beg ch1 [9]

Rnd 7: ch1, sc4, sc3 in next st, sc4, slst in beg ch1 [11]

Rnd 8: ch1, sc5, sc3 in next st, sc5, slst in beg ch1 [13]

Rnds 9–10: ch1, sc1 in each st, slst in beg ch1 (2 rnds)

Fasten off.

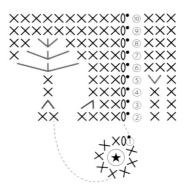

Muzzle (make 1)

With Yarn A, make 3ch.

Rnd 1: skip first ch, sc1 in next ch, sc3 in last ch, rotate and work along opposite side of chain, sc2 in next ch, slst in skipped ch at beg of rnd [6]

Place stitch marker in first st of rnd 1 and move it up after each round

Rnd 2: ch1, (sc2, sc2 in next st) twice, slst in beg ch1 [8]

Rnd 3: ch1, sc1 in each st to end, slst in beg ch1

Rnd 4: ch1, sc4, (sc2 in next st) twice, sc2, slst in beg ch1 [10]

Rnd 5: ch1, sc5, (sc2 in next st) twice, sc3, slst in beg ch1 [12]

Fasten off.

Add toy safety nose at position shown in diagram, at center front of muzzle, between rnds 1 and 2.

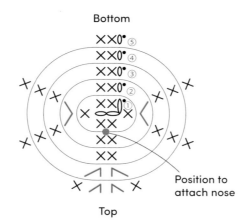

Bottom

Position to attach nose

Top

Tail (make 1)

With Yarn A, make a magic ring.

Rnd 1: ch1 (does not count as a st throughout), sc5 in magic ring, slst in beg ch1 [5]

Place stitch marker in first st of rnd 1 and move it up after each round

Rnd 2: ch1, sc4, sc2 in last st, slst in beg ch1 [6]

Rnds 3–7: ch1, sc1 in each st, slst in beg ch1 (5 rnds)

Fasten off.

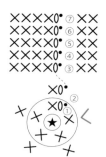

GRAFTING & FINISHING

Location	Yarn Used	Yarn Length
Head		1¼"–2¾" (3–7 cm)
Body		1¼"–2¾" (3–7 cm)
Tail	B	3½" (9 cm)
Muzzle		¾" (2 cm)
Legs		1½" (4 cm)

FINISHED SIZE

8¼" (21 cm) tall × 13" (33 cm) long

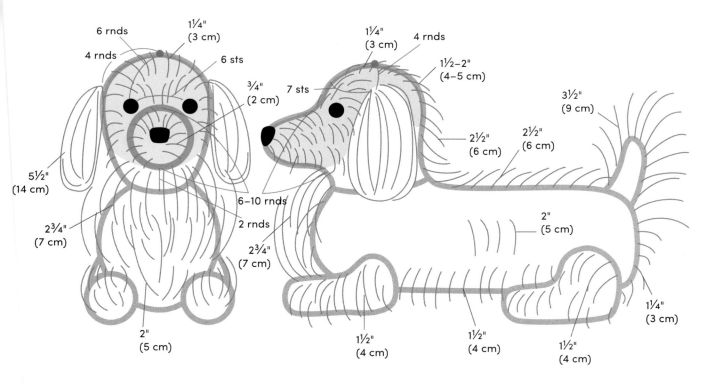

- For grafting, always use a total of 4 strands (2 of the sport weight acrylic and 2 of the light fingering weight acrylic/mohair blend).
- Refer to instructions on page 60 to make the ears with wrapped yarn. Use a 5½" (14 cm) long piece of cardboard.
- ▢ = Needle felt the areas shaded in light blue in order to compress the yarn and shape the head.

Dachshund / Stand

TOOLS & MATERIALS

- P/15 (10 mm) crochet hook
- 276 yds (210 g) bulky weight acrylic yarn in dark brown
- 66 yds (50 g) bulky weight acrylic yarn in dark beige
- 355 yds (90 g) sport weight acrylic yarn in dark brown
- 40 yds (10 g) sport weight acrylic yarn in golden brown
- 350 yds (80 g) of light fingering weight acrylic/mohair blend yarn in dark brown
- 44 yds (10 g) of light fingering weight acrylic/mohair blend yarn in brown
- Pair of 15 mm black plastic toy safety eyes

- One 20 mm black plastic toy safety nose
- Polyester fiber fill toy stuffing (about 60 g)
- Stitch marker
- Yarn needle
- Felting needle
- Slicker brush

YARN COMBINATION CHART

Use		Yarn Type	Yarn Color	Strands
Crocheting the Foundation	A	Bulky weight acrylic	Dark brown	2 strands
	B	Bulky weight acrylic	Dark beige	2 strands
Grafting the Fur	C	Sport weight acrylic	Dark brown	2 strands
		Light fingering weight acrylic/mohair blend	Dark brown	2 strands
	D	Sport weight acrylic	Golden brown	2 strands
		Light fingering weight acrylic/mohair blend	Brown	2 strands

CONSTRUCTION STEPS

1. Crochet the body, head, front legs, back legs, ears, muzzle, and tail following instructions on pages 101–102 (also see pages 45–52).

2. Stuff and assemble the body parts following the instructions for the stand pose on pages 54–55.

Front   Side   Back

3. Graft yarn according to the lengths listed on page 103 (refer to pages 56–58 for general grafting instructions).

4. Follow the techniques on page 58 to loosen the yarn and trim the fur into shape. Use the photos below as a reference.

CROCHET INSTRUCTIONS

Crochet Symbol Key

★ = magic ring   ∧ = ⩚ = sc2tog   ⋁ = 3 single crochet increase

0 = ch st   ⋁ = ⩚ = sc2 in next st   ⋀ = 3 single crochet decrease

• = slst

Yarn Color Key

� = Yarn A

▓ = Yarn B

Body (make 1)

With Yarn A, make a magic ring.

Rnd 1: ch1 (does not count as a st throughout), sc6 in magic ring, slst in beg ch1 [6]

Place stitch marker in first st of rnd 1 and move it up after each round.

Rnd 2: ch1, (sc2 in next st) 6 times, slst in beg ch1 [12]

Rnd 3: ch1, (sc1, sc2 in next st) 6 times, slst in beg ch1 [18]

Rnd 4: ch1, (sc2, sc2 in next st) 6 times, slst in beg ch1 [24]

Rnds 5–30: ch1, sc1 in each st, slst in beg ch1 (26 rnds)

Rnd 31: ch1, (sc2, sc2tog) 6 times, slst in beg ch1 [18] Begin to stuff body firmly.

Rnd 32: ch1, (sc1, sc2tog) 6 times, slst in beg ch1 [12]

Rnd 33: ch1, (sc2tog) 6 times, slst in beg ch1 [6]

Fasten off leaving a long tail end. Add more stuffing if needed then thread yarn through stitches of last round and pull tightly to close.

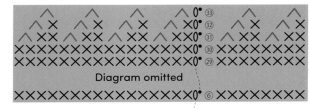

Front   Thread through 6 sts in the last round and gather (stuff before closing)

Diagram omitted

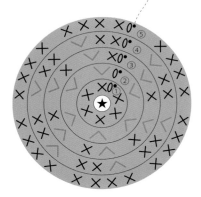

Head (make 1)

With Yarn A, make a magic ring.

Rnd 1: ch1 (does not count as a st throughout), sc6 in magic ring, slst in beg ch1 [6]

Place stitch marker in first st of rnd 1 and move it up after each round

Rnd 2: ch1, (sc2 in next st) 6 times, slst in beg ch1 [12]

Rnd 3: ch1, (sc1, sc2 in next st) 6 times, slst in beg ch1 [18]

Rnd 4: ch1, (sc2, sc2 in next st) 6 times, slst in beg ch1 [24]

Rnds 5–9: ch1, sc1 in each st, slst in beg ch1 (5 rnds)

Rnd 10: ch1, sc8, sc2tog, sc4, sc2tog, sc8, slst in beg ch1 [22]

Rnd 11: ch1, sc4, (sc2tog, sc2) 3 times, sc2tog, sc4, slst in beg ch1 [18]

Rnd 12: ch1, sc1, sc2 in next st, sc14, sc2 in next st, sc1, slst in beg ch1 [20]

Fasten off.

Attach toy safety eyes to front of face at position shown in diagram on page 103, between rnds 6 and 7, leaving 6 sts between eyes.

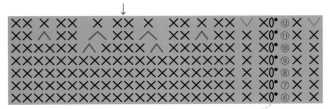

Center front
↓

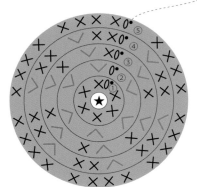

Front Legs (make 2)

With Yarn B, make a magic ring.

Rnd 1: ch1 (does not count as a st throughout), sc8 in magic ring, slst in beg ch1 [8]

Place stitch marker in first st of rnd 1 and move it up after each round

Rnd 2: ch1, sc1 in each st, slst in beg ch1

Rnd 3: ch1, sc2, (sc2tog) twice, sc2, slst in beg ch1 [6]

Rnds 4–5: ch1, sc1 in each st, slst in beg ch1 (2 rnds)

Change to Yarn A

Rnd 6: ch1, sc5, sc2 in next st, slst in beg ch1 [7]

Rnd 7: ch1, sc6, sc2 in next st, slst in beg ch1 [8]

Rnd 8: ch1, sc7, sc2 in next st, slst in beg ch1 [9]

Rnd 9: ch1, sc8, sc2 in next st, slst in beg ch1 [10]

Fasten off.

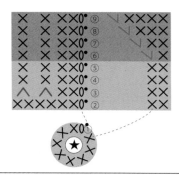

Back Legs (make 2)

With Yarn B, make a magic ring.

Rnd 1: ch1 (does not count as a st throughout), sc8 in magic ring, slst in beg ch1 [8]

Place stitch marker in first st of rnd 1 and move it up after each round

Rnd 2: ch1, sc1 in each st, slst in beg ch1

Rnd 3: ch1, sc2, (sc2tog) twice, sc2, slst in beg ch1 [6]

Rnd 4: ch1, sc1 in each st, slst in beg ch1

Rnd 5: ch1, sc5, sc2 in next st, slst in beg ch1 [7]

Change to Yarn A

Rnd 6: ch1, sc3, sc3 in next st, sc3, slst in beg ch1 [9]

Rnd 7: ch1, sc4, sc3 in next st, sc4, slst in beg ch1 [11]

Rnd 8: ch1, sc5, sc3 in next st, sc5, slst in beg ch1 [13]

Rnds 9–10: ch1, sc1 in each st, slst in beg ch1 (2 rnds)

Fasten off.

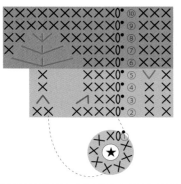

Ears (make 2)

With Yarn A, make 4ch, leaving a 12" (30 cm) tail of yarn.

Work in rows.

Row 1: sc1 in second ch from hook, sc1 in each remaining ch, turn [3]

Row 2: ch1 (does not count as a st throughout), sc2 in first st, sc1, sc2 in last st, turn [5]

Rows 3–6: ch1, sc1 in each st to end, turn (4 rows)

Row 7: ch1, sc2tog, sc1, sc2tog, turn [3]

Row 8: ch1, sc3tog [1]

Fasten off.

Bottom

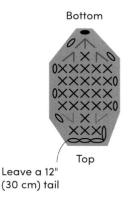

Top

Leave a 12"
(30 cm) tail

Muzzle (make 1)

With Yarn B, make 3ch.

Rnd 1: skip first ch, sc1 in next ch, sc3 in last ch, rotate and work along opposite side of chain, sc2 in next ch, slst in skipped ch at beg of rnd [6]

Place stitch marker in first st of rnd 1 and move it up after each round

Join in Yarn A when needed.

Rnd 2: ch1, in Yarn B sc2, sc2 in next st, in Yarn A sc2, in Yarn B sc2 in next st, slst in beg ch1 [8]

Rnd 3: ch1, in Yarn B sc4, in Yarn A sc2, in Yarn B sc2, slst in beg ch1

Rnd 4: ch1, in Yarn B sc4, in Yarn B sc1 in next st, change to Yarn A and sc1 in same st, in Yarn A sc1 in next st, change to Yarn B and sc1 in same st, in Yarn B sc2, slst in beg ch1 [10]

Rnd 5: ch1, in Yarn B sc5, in Yarn B sc1 in next st, change to Yarn A and sc1 in same st, in Yarn A sc1 in next st, change to Yarn B and sc1 in same st, in Yarn B sc3, slst in beg ch1 [12]

Fasten off.

Add toy safety nose at position shown in diagram, at center front of muzzle, between rnds 1 and 2.

Bottom

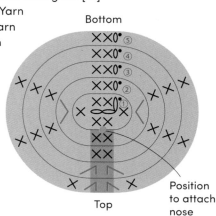

Top

Position to attach nose

Tail (make 1)

With Yarn A, make a magic ring.
Rnd 1: ch1 (does not count as a st throughout), sc5 in magic ring, slst in beg ch1 [5]
Place stitch marker in first st of rnd 1 and move it up after each round
Rnd 2: ch1, sc4, sc2 in last st, slst in beg ch1 [6]
Rnds 3–7: ch1, sc1 in each st, slst in beg ch1 (5 rnds)
Fasten off.

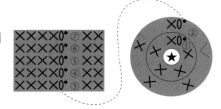

GRAFTING & FINISHING

Location	Yarn Used	Yarn Length
Head	C, D	¾"–2¾" (2–7 cm)
Body	C, D	1¼"–2¾" (3–6 cm)
Tail	C	3½" (9 cm)
Muzzle	C, D	¾" (2 cm)
Legs	C	1¼"–1½" (3–4 cm) (base only)
Ears	C	2"–2¾" (5–7 cm)

FINISHED SIZE

9½" (24 cm) tall × 13" (33 cm) long

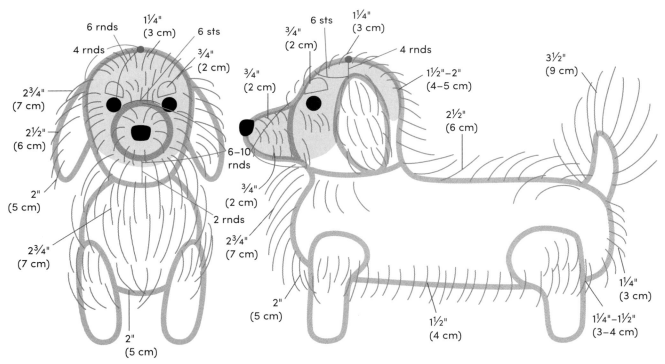

- For grafting, always use a total of 4 strands (2 of the sport weight acrylic and 2 of the light fingering weight acrylic/mohair blend).
- Refer to page 59 for instructions on embroidering and needle felting the eyebrows.
- ▢ = Needle felt the areas shaded in light blue in order to compress the yarn and shape the head.
- Graft the chest fur and the base of the legs with Yarn D as desired.

Maltese / Sit

Shown on page 30

TOOLS & MATERIALS

- P/15 (10 mm) crochet hook
- 289 yds (220 g) bulky weight acrylic yarn in white
- 394 yds (100 g) sport weight acrylic yarn in white
- 394 yds (90 g) of light fingering weight acrylic/mohair blend yarn in white

- Pair of 18 mm black plastic toy safety eyes
- One 21 mm black plastic toy safety nose
- Polyester fiber fill toy stuffing (about 50 g)
- Stitch marker
- Yarn needle
- Felting needle
- Slicker brush

YARN COMBINATION CHART

Area		Yarn Used	Yarn Color	Strands
Crocheting the Foundation	A	Bulky weight acrylic	White	2 strands
Grafting the Fur	B	Sport weight acrylic	White	2 strands
		Light fingering weight acrylic/mohair blend	White	2 strands

CONSTRUCTION STEPS

1. Crochet the body, head, front legs, back legs, ears, muzzle, and tail following instructions on pages 105–107 (also see pages 45–52).

2. Stuff and assemble the body parts following the instructions for the sit pose on pages 53–55.

3. Graft yarn according to the lengths listed on page 108 (refer to pages 56–58 for general grafting instructions).

4. Follow the techniques on page 58 to loosen the yarn and trim the fur into shape. Use the photos below as a reference.

Front   Side   Back

CROCHET INSTRUCTIONS

Crochet Symbol Key

★ = magic ring ∧ = ⋀ = sc2tog ∨ = 3 single crochet increase

0 = ch st ∨ = ⋓ = sc2 in next st ⋙ = 5 single crochet increase

• = slst

Body (make 1)

With Yarn A, make a magic ring.

Rnd 1: ch1 (does not count as a st throughout), sc6 in magic ring, slst in beg ch1 [6]

Place stitch marker in first st of rnd 1 and move it up after each round

Rnd 2: ch1, (sc2 in next st) 6 times, slst in beg ch1 [12]

Rnd 3: ch1, (sc1, sc2 in next st) 6 times, slst in beg ch1 [18]

Rnd 4: ch1, (sc2, sc2 in next st) 6 times, slst in beg ch1 [24]

Rnd 5: ch1, sc2 in first st, sc22, sc2 in last st, slst in beg ch1 [26]

Rnds 6–9: ch1, sc1 in each st, slst in beg ch1 (4 rnds)

Rnd 10: ch1, sc1, sc2tog, sc20, sc2tog, sc1, slst in beg ch1 [24]

Rnd 11: ch1, sc1 in each st, slst in beg ch1

Rnd 12: ch1, sc1, sc2tog, sc18, sc2tog, sc1, slst in beg ch1 [22]

Rnd 13: ch1, sc1 in each st, slst in beg ch1

Rnd 14: ch1, sc1, sc2tog, sc5, sc2 in next st, sc4, sc2 in next st, sc5, sc2tog, sc1, slst in beg ch1 [22]

Rnds 15–18: ch1, sc1 in each st, slst in beg ch1 (4 rnds)

Rnd 19: as rnd 14

Rnds 20–22: ch1, sc1 in each st, slst in beg ch1 (3 rnds)

Rnd 23: ch1, sc1, (sc2tog, sc4) 3 times, sc2tog, sc1, slst in beg ch1 [18]

Fasten off.

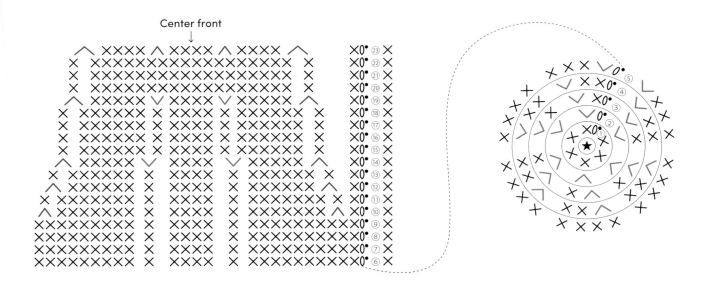

Center front

Head (make 1)

With Yarn A, make a magic ring.

Rnd 1: ch1 (does not count as a st throughout), sc6 in magic ring, slst in beg ch1 [6]

Place stitch marker in first st of rnd 1 and move it up after each round

Rnd 2: ch1, (sc2 in next st) 6 times, slst in beg ch1 [12]

Rnd 3: ch1, (sc1, sc2 in next st) 6 times, slst in beg ch1 [18]

Rnd 4: ch1, (sc2, sc2 in next st) 6 times, slst in beg ch1 [24]

Rnds 5–9: ch1, sc1 in each st, slst in beg ch1 (5 rnds)

Rnd 10: ch1, sc8, sc2tog, sc4, sc2tog, sc8, slst in beg ch1 [22]

Rnd 11: ch1, sc4, (sc2tog, sc2) 3 times, sc2tog, sc4, slst in beg ch1 [18]

Rnd 12: ch1, sc1 in each st, slst in beg ch1

Fasten off.

Attach toy safety eyes to front of face at position shown in diagram on page 108, between rnds 6 and 7, leaving 5 sts between eyes.

Center front
↓

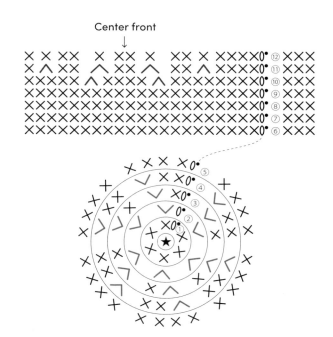

Front Legs (make 2)

With Yarn A, make a magic ring.

Rnd 1: ch1 (does not count as a st throughout), sc7 in magic ring, slst in beg ch1 [7]

Place stitch marker in first st of rnd 1 and move it up after each round

Rnds 2–8: ch1, sc1 in each st, slst in beg ch1 (7 rnds)

Rnd 9: ch1, sc6, sc2 in last st, slst in beg ch1 [8]

Rnd 10: ch1, sc1 in each st, slst in beg ch1

Rnd 11: ch1, sc7, sc2 in last st, slst in beg ch1 [9]

Rnd 12: ch1, sc8, sc2 in last st, slst in beg ch1 [10]

Rnd 13: ch1, sc9, sc2 in last st, slst in beg ch1 [11]

Fasten off.

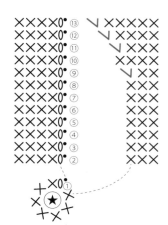

Back Legs (make 2)

With Yarn A, make a magic ring.

Rnd 1: ch1 (does not count as a st throughout), sc7 in magic ring, slst in beg ch1 [7]

Place stitch marker in first st of rnd 1 and move it up after each round

Rnds 2–7: ch1, sc1 in each st, slst in beg ch1 (6 rnds)

Rnd 8: ch1, sc3, sc5 in next st, sc3, slst in beg ch1 [11]

Rnd 9: ch1, sc5, sc5 in next st, sc5, slst in beg ch1 [15]

Rnd 10: ch1, sc7, sc3 in next st, sc7, slst in beg ch1 [17]

Rnds 11–12: ch1, sc1 in each st, slst in beg ch1 (2 rnds)

Rnd 13: ch1, sc6, sc2tog, sc1, sc2tog, sc6, slst in beg ch1 [15]

Fasten off.

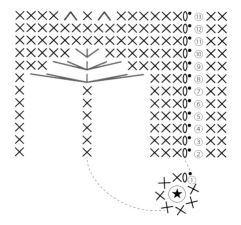

Ears (make 2)

With Yarn A, make 4ch, leaving a 12" (30 cm) tail of yarn.

Work in rows.

Row 1: sc1 in second ch from hook, sc1 in each remaining ch, turn [3]

Row 2: ch1 (does not count as a st throughout), sc2 in first st, sc1, sc2 in last st, turn [5]

Rows 3–4: ch1, sc1 in each st to end, turn

Fasten off.

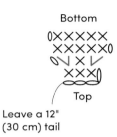

Bottom

Top

Leave a 12"
(30 cm) tail

Muzzle (make 1)

With Yarn A, make 5ch.

Rnd 1: skip first ch, sc1 in next ch, sc1 in next 2 ch, sc3 in last ch, rotate and work along opposite side of chain, sc1 in next 2 ch, sc2 in next ch, slst in skipped ch at beg of rnd [10]

Place stitch marker in first st of rnd 1 and move it up after each round

Rnd 2: ch1, (sc4, sc2 in next st) twice, slst in beg ch1 [12]

Rnds 3–4: ch1, sc1 in each st, slst in beg ch1

Fasten off.

Add toy safety nose at position shown in diagram, at center front of muzzle, between rnds 1 and 2.

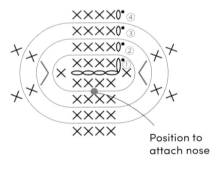

Position to
attach nose

Tail (make 1)

With Yarn A, make a magic ring.

Rnd 1: ch1 (does not count as a st throughout), sc5 in magic ring, slst in beg ch1 [5]

Place stitch marker in first st of rnd 1 and move it up after each round

Rnd 2: ch1, sc4, sc2 in last st, slst in beg ch1 [6]

Rnds 3–7: ch1, sc1 in each st, slst in beg ch1 (5 rnds)

Fasten off.

GRAFTING & FINISHING

Location	Yarn Used	Yarn Length
Head		1¼"–1½" (3–4 cm)
Body		1½" (4 cm)
Tail		2" (5 cm)
Muzzle	B	1¼"–2" (3–5 cm)
Legs		1½" (3.5 cm)
Ears		2½" (6 cm)

FINISHED SIZE

11¾" (30 cm) tall × 8" (20 cm) long

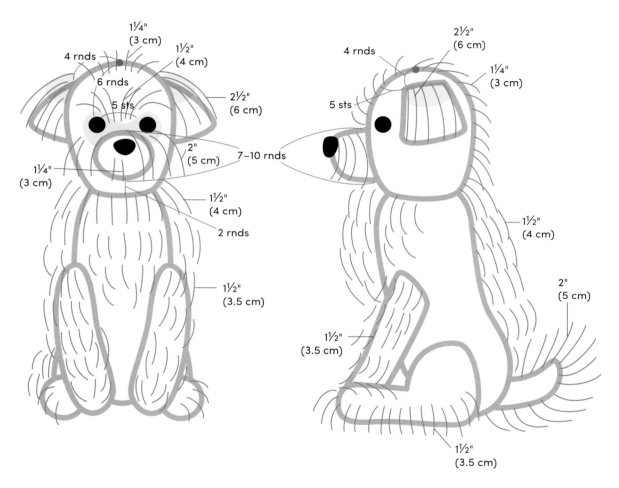

- For grafting, always use a total of 4 strands (2 of the sport weight acrylic and 2 of the light fingering weight acrylic/mohair blend).
- Achieving the proper flow of fur is more important than loosening the yarn.
- ▢ = Needle felt the areas shaded in light blue in order to compress the yarn and shape the head.
- Adjust the length of the ears and fur as desired.

Miniature Schnauzer / Sit

TOOLS & MATERIALS

- P/15 (10 mm) crochet hook
- 418 yds (280 g) bulky weight acrylic yarn in gray
- 194 yds (130 g) bulky weight acrylic yarn in white
- Pair of 15 mm black plastic toy safety eyes
- One 23 mm black plastic toy safety nose
- Polyester fiber fill toy stuffing (about 50 g)
- Stitch marker
- Yarn needle
- Felting needle
- Slicker brush

YARN COMBINATION CHART

Area	Yarn Used		Yarn Color	Amount	Strands
Crocheting the Foundation	A	Bulky weight acrylic	Gray	298 yds (200 g)	2 strands
	B	Bulky weight acrylic	White	149 yds (100 g)	2 strands
Grafting the Fur	C	Bulky weight acrylic	Gray	120 yds (80 g)	2 strands
	D	Bulky weight acrylic	White	45 yds (30 g)	2 strands

CONSTRUCTION STEPS

1. Crochet the body, head, front legs, back legs, ears, muzzle, and tail following instructions on pages 110–112 (also see pages 45–52).

2. Stuff and assemble the body parts following the instructions for the sit pose on pages 53–55.

3. Graft yarn according to the lengths listed on page 113 (refer to pages 56–58 for general grafting instructions).

4. Follow the techniques on page 58 to loosen the yarn and trim the fur into shape. Use the photos below as a reference.

Front

Side

Back

CROCHET INSTRUCTIONS

Crochet Symbol Key

★ = magic ring
0 = ch st
• = slst
∧ = ⩓ = sc2tog
∨ = ⩔ = sc2 in next st
⩛ = 3 single crochet increase
⩛ = 5 single crochet increase

Yarn Color Key

(shaded) = Yarn A
(white) = Yarn B

Body (make 1)

With Yarn A, make a magic ring.

Rnd 1: ch1 (does not count as a st throughout), sc6 in magic ring, slst in beg ch1 [6]

Place stitch marker in first st of rnd 1 and move it up after each round

Rnd 2: ch1, (sc2 in next st) 6 times, slst in beg ch1 [12]

Rnd 3: ch1, (sc1, sc2 in next st) 6 times, slst in beg ch1 [18]

Rnd 4: ch1, (sc2, sc2 in next st) 6 times, slst in beg ch1 [24]

Join Yarn B (2 strands held together) on next round when needed

Rnd 5: In Yarn A ch1, sc2 in next st, sc9, in Yarn B sc4, in Yarn A sc9, sc2 in next st, slst in beg ch1 [26]

Rnd 6: in Yarn A ch1, sc11, in Yarn B sc4, in Yarn A sc11, slst in beg ch1

Rnds 7–9: in Yarn A ch1, sc10, in Yarn B sc6, in Yarn A sc10, slst in beg ch1 (3 rnds)

Rnd 10: in Yarn A ch1, sc1, sc2tog, sc7, in Yarn B sc6, in Yarn A sc7, sc2tog, sc1, slst in beg ch1 [24]

Rnd 11: in Yarn A ch1, sc9, in Yarn B sc6, in Yarn A sc9, slst in beg ch1

Rnd 12: in Yarn A ch1, sc1, sc2tog, sc6, in Yarn B sc6, in Yarn A sc6, sc2tog, sc1, slst in beg ch1 [22]

Rnd 13: in Yarn A ch1, sc8, in Yarn B sc6, in Yarn A sc8, slst in beg ch1

Rnd 14: in Yarn A ch1, sc1, sc2tog, sc5, sc2 in next st, sc4, sc2 in next st, sc5, sc2tog, sc1, slst in beg ch1 [22]

Rnd 15: in Yarn A ch1, sc1 in each st, slst in beg ch1

Rnd 16: in Yarn A ch1, sc10, in Yarn B sc2, in Yarn A sc10, slst in beg ch1

Rnds 17–18: in Yarn A ch1, sc8, in Yarn B sc6, in Yarn A sc8, slst in beg ch1 (2 rnds)

Rnd 19: in Yarn A ch1, sc1, sc2tog, sc5, in Yarn B sc2 in next st, sc1, in Yarn A sc2, in Yarn B sc1, sc2 in next st, in Yarn A sc5, sc2tog, sc1, slst in beg ch1 [22]

Continue in Yarn A only

Rnds 20–22: ch1, sc1 in each st, slst in beg ch1 (3 rnds)

Rnd 23: ch1, sc1, (sc2tog, sc4) 3 times, sc2tog, sc1, slst in beg ch1 [18]

Fasten off.

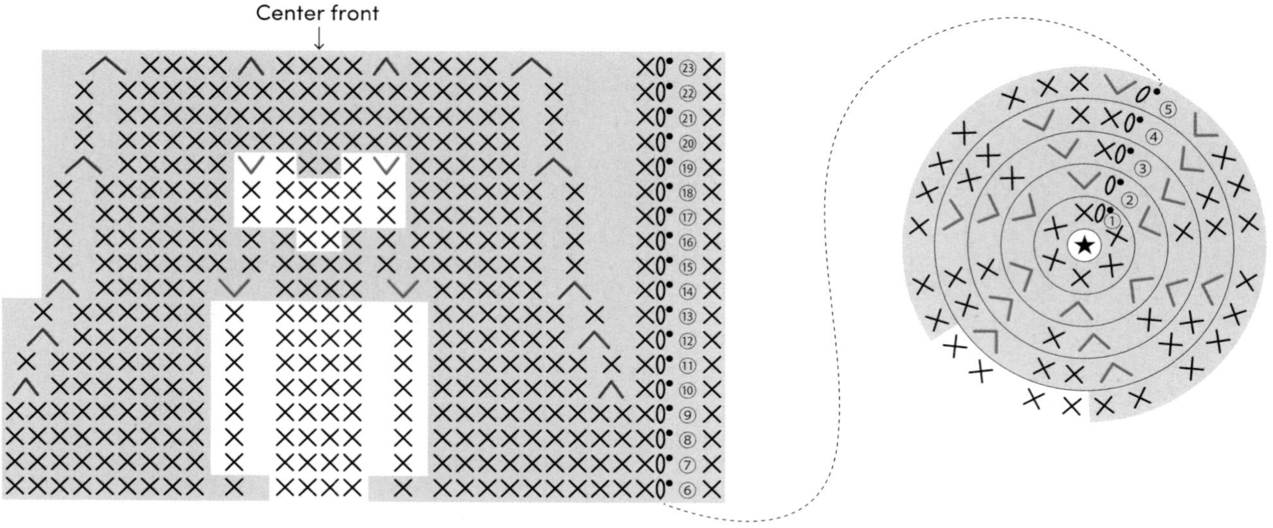

Head (make 1)

With Yarn A, make a magic ring.

Rnd 1: ch1 (does not count as a st throughout), sc6 in magic ring, slst in beg ch1 [6]

Place stitch marker in first st of rnd 1 and move it up after each round

Rnd 2: ch1, (sc2 in next st) 6 times, slst in beg ch1 [12]

Rnd 3: ch1, (sc1, sc2 in next st) 6 times, slst in beg ch1 [18]

Rnd 4: ch1, (sc2, sc2 in next st) 6 times, slst in beg ch1 [24]

Rnds 5–9: ch1, sc1 in each st, slst in beg ch1 (5 rnds)

Rnd 10: ch1, sc8, sc2tog, sc4, sc2tog, sc8, slst in beg ch1 [22]

Rnd 11: ch1, sc4, (sc2tog, sc2) 3 times, sc2tog, sc4, slst beg ch1 [18]

Rnd 12: ch1, sc1 in each st, slst in beg ch1

Fasten off.

Attach toy safety eyes to front of face at position shown in diagram on page 113, between rnds 5 and 6, leaving 6 sts between eyes.

Center front

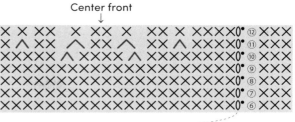

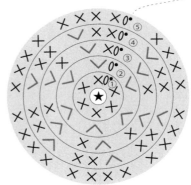

Front Legs (make 2)

With Yarn B, make a magic ring.

Rnd 1: ch1 (does not count as a st throughout), sc7 in magic ring, slst in beg ch1 [7]

Place stitch marker in first st of rnd 1 and move it up after each round

Rnds 2–7: ch1, sc1 in each st, slst in beg ch1 (6 rnds)

Change to Yarn A

Rnd 8: ch1, sc1 in each st, slst in beg ch1

Rnd 9: ch1, sc6, sc2 in next st, slst in beg ch1 [8]

Rnd 10: ch1, sc1 in each st to end, slst in beg ch1

Rnd 11: ch1, sc7, sc2 in next st, slst in beg ch1 [9]

Rnd 12: ch1, sc8, sc2 in next st, slst in beg ch1 [10]

Rnd 13: ch1, sc9, sc2 in next st, slst in beg ch1 [11]

Fasten off.

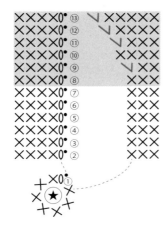

Back Legs (make 2)

With Yarn B, make a magic ring.

Rnd 1: ch1 (does not count as a st throughout), sc7 in magic ring, slst in beg ch1 [7]

Place stitch marker in first st of rnd 1 and move it up after each round

Rnds 2–6: ch1, sc1 in each st, slst in beg ch1 (5 rnds)

Change to Yarn A

Rnd 7: ch1, sc1 in each st, slst in beg ch1

Rnd 8: ch1, sc3, sc5 in next st, sc3, slst in beg ch1 [11]

Rnd 9: ch1, sc5, sc5 in next st, sc5, slst in beg ch1 [15]

Rnd 10: ch1, sc7, sc3 in next st, sc7, slst in beg ch1 [17]

Rnds 11–12: ch1, sc1 in each st, slst in beg ch1 (2 rnds)

Rnd 13: ch1, sc6, sc2tog, sc1, sc2tog, sc6, slst in beg ch1 [15]

Fasten off.

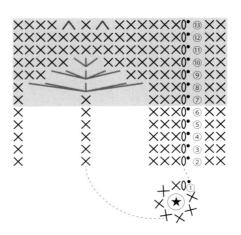

Ears (make 2)

With Yarn A, make a magic ring.

Rnd 1: ch1 (does not count as a st throughout), sc5 in magic ring, slst in beg ch1 [5]

Place stitch marker in first st of rnd 1 and move it up after each round

Join Yarn B on next round when needed

Rnd 2: in Yarn A ch1, (in Yarn A sc2 in next st, in Yarn B sc2 in next st) twice, in Yarn A sc2 in next st, slst in beg ch1 [10]

Rnd 3: in Yarn A ch1, sc2 in first st, in Yarn B sc3, in Yarn A sc2, in Yarn B sc3, in Yarn A sc2 in next st, slst in beg ch1 [12]

Rnd 4: in Yarn A ch1, sc2 in first st, in Yarn B sc4, in Yarn A sc2, in Yarn B sc4, in Yarn A sc2 in next st, slst in beg ch1 [14]

Rnd 5: in Yarn A ch1, sc2 in first st, in Yarn B sc5, in Yarn A sc2, in Yarn B sc5, in Yarn A sc2 in next st, slst in beg ch1 [16]

Rnd 6: in Yarn A ch1, sc2 in first st, in Yarn B sc6, in Yarn A sc2, in Yarn B sc6, in Yarn A sc2 in next st, slst in beg ch1 [18]

Rnd 7: in Yarn A ch1, sc2 in first st, in Yarn B sc7, in Yarn A sc2, in Yarn B sc7, in Yarn A sc2 in next st, slst in beg ch1 [20]

Rnds 8–13: in Yarn A ch1, sc2, in Yarn B sc7, in Yarn A sc2, in Yarn B sc7, in Yarn A sc2, slst in beg ch1

Fasten off.

To make second ear, switch the colors, using Yarn B instead of Yarn A and vice versa.

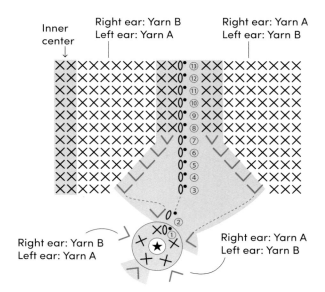

Inner center

Right ear: Yarn B
Left ear: Yarn A

Right ear: Yarn A
Left ear: Yarn B

Right ear: Yarn B
Left ear: Yarn A

Right ear: Yarn A
Left ear: Yarn B

Muzzle (make 1)

With Yarn B, make 5ch.

Rnd 1: skip first ch, sc1 in next ch, sc1 in next 2 ch, sc3 in last ch, rotate and work along opposite side of chain, sc1 in next 2 ch, sc2 in last ch, slst in skipped ch at beg of rnd [10]

Place stitch marker in first st of rnd 1 and move it up after each round

Rnd 2: ch1, (sc4, sc2 in next st) twice, slst in beg ch1 [12]

Rnds 3–4: ch1, sc1 in each st, slst in beg ch1 (2 rnds)

Fasten off.

Add toy safety nose at position shown in diagram, at center front of muzzle, between rnds 1 and 2.

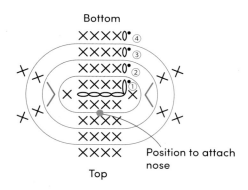

Bottom

Position to attach nose

Top

Tail (make 1)

With Yarn A, make a magic ring.

Rnd 1: ch1 (does not count as a st throughout), sc5 in magic ring, slst in beg ch1 [5]

Place stitch marker in first st of rnd 1 and move it up after each round

Rnd 2: ch1, sc4, sc2 in last st, slst in beg ch1 [6]

Rnds 3–5: ch1, sc1 in each st, slst in beg ch1 (3 rnds)

Fasten off.

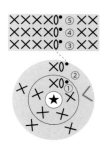

GRAFTING & FINISHING

Location	Yarn Used	Yarn Length
Head	C, D	¾" (2 cm)
Body	C, D	1¼"–1½" (3–4 cm)
Tail		No grafting
Muzzle	D	¾"–1¼" (2–3 cm)
Legs	C, D	1½" (3.5 cm)
Ears		No grafting

FINISHED SIZE

11¾" (30 cm) tall × 8" (20 cm) long

Eyebrow Placement

Refer to page 59 for more detailed instructions on making the eyebrows.

 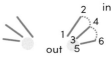

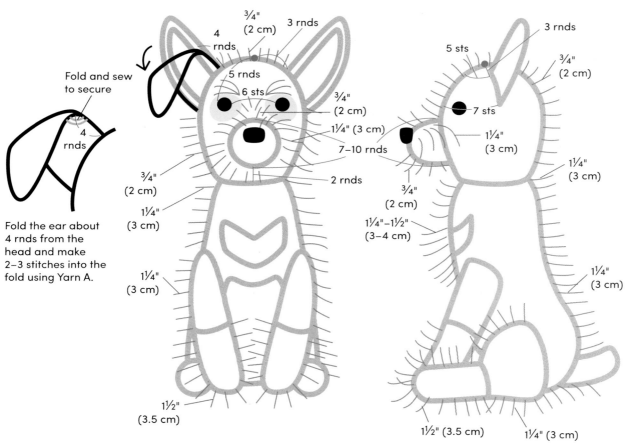

Fold and sew to secure

4 rnds

Fold the ear about 4 rnds from the head and make 2–3 stitches into the fold using Yarn A.

¾" (2 cm)
4 rnds
3 rnds
5 rnds
6 sts
¾" (2 cm)
1¼" (3 cm)
7–10 rnds
2 rnds
¾" (2 cm)
1¼" (3 cm)
1¼" (3 cm)
1½" (3.5 cm)

3 rnds
5 sts
¾" (2 cm)
7 sts
1¼" (3 cm)
1¼" (3 cm)
¾" (2 cm)
1¼"–1½" (3–4 cm)
1¼" (3 cm)
1½" (3.5 cm)
1¼" (3 cm)

- Use total 4 stands (2 strands each) or 2 strands of acrylic bulky yarn.
- Attach the ears so that the front side is white.
- Brush the front and back with a slicker brush before grafting the ears and tail.
- Graft on the eyebrows and then needle felt the yarn (refer to the photo above for reference).
- ▢ = Graft Yarn D between the eyebrows, directly above the muzzle, to create a Schnauzer-like look.
- ▢ = Needle felt the areas shaded in light blue in order to compress the yarn and shape the head.

TOOLS & MATERIALS

- P/15 (10 mm) crochet hook
- 289 yds (220 g) bulky weight acrylic yarn in off-white
- 394 yds (100 g) sport weight acrylic yarn in off-white
- 40 yds (10 g) of sport weight acrylic yarn in dark beige
- 394 yds (90 g) of light fingering weight acrylic/mohair blend yarn in off-white
- 44 yds (10 g) of light fingering weight acrylic/mohair blend yarn in dark gray
- 44 yds (10 g) of light fingering weight acrylic/mohair blend yarn in sand beige
- 44 yds (10 g) of light fingering weight acrylic/mohair blend yarn in brown
- Pair of 18 mm black plastic toy safety eyes
- One 20 mm black plastic toy safety nose
- Polyester fiber fill toy stuffing (about 50 g)
- Stitch marker
- Yarn needle
- Felting needle
- Slicker brush

YARN COMBINATION CHART

Use	Yarn Type		Yarn Color	Strands
Crocheting the Foundation	A	Bulky weight acrylic	Off-white	2 strands
Grafting the Fur	B	Sport weight acrylic	Off-white	2 strands
		Light fingering weight acrylic/mohair blend	Off-white	2 strands
	C	Sport weight acrylic	Dark beige	1 strand
		Light fingering weight acrylic/mohair blend	Dark gray	1 strand
		Light fingering weight acrylic/mohair blend	Sand beige	1 strand
		Light fingering weight acrylic/mohair blend	Brown	1 strand

CONSTRUCTION STEPS

1. Crochet the body, head, front legs, back legs, muzzle, and tail following instructions on pages 115–116 (also see pages 45–52). Make the ears as shown on page 60.

Front   Side   Back

2. Stuff and assemble the body parts following the instructions for the lie down pose on pages 54–55.

3. Graft yarn according to the lengths listed on page 117 (refer to pages 56–58 for general grafting instructions).

4. Follow the techniques on page 58 to loosen the yarn and trim the fur into shape. Use the photos at right as a reference.

CROCHET INSTRUCTIONS

Crochet Symbol Key

★ = magic ring   ∧ = 🔺 = sc2tog   𝗏 = 3 single crochet increase

0 = ch st   ∨ = 𝗪 = sc2 in next st   𝗪 = 5 single crochet increase

• = slst

Body (make 1)

With Yarn A, make a magic ring.

Rnd 1: ch1 (does not count as a st throughout), sc6 in magic ring, slst in beg ch1 [6]

Place stitch marker in first st of rnd 1 and move it up after each round

Rnd 2: ch1, (sc2 in next st) 6 times, slst in beg ch1 [12]

Rnd 3: ch1, (sc1, sc2 in next st) 6 times, slst in beg ch1 [18]

Rnd 4: ch1, (sc2, sc2 in next st) 6 times, slst in beg ch1 [24]

Rnds 5–24: ch1, sc1 in each st, slst in beg ch1 (20 rnds)

Rnd 25: ch1, (sc2, sc2tog) 6 times, slst in beg ch1 [18]

Begin to stuff body firmly.

Rnd 26: ch1, (sc1, sc2tog) 6 times, slst in beg ch1 [12]

Rnd 27: ch1, (sc2tog) 6 times, slst in beg ch1 [6]

Fasten off leaving a long tail end. Add more stuffing if needed then thread yarn through stitches of last round and pull tightly to close.

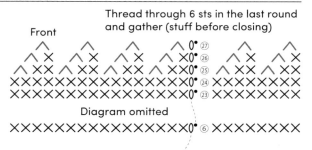

Thread through 6 sts in the last round and gather (stuff before closing)

Front

Diagram omitted

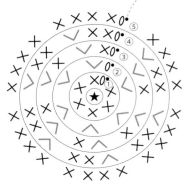

Muzzle (make 1)

With Yarn A, make 5ch.

Rnd 1: skip first ch, sc1 in next ch, sc1 in next 2 ch, sc3 in last ch, rotate and work along opposite side of chain, sc1 in next 2 ch, sc2 in next ch, slst in skipped ch at beg of rnd [10]

Place stitch marker in first st of rnd 1 and move it up after each round

Rnd 2: ch1, (sc4, sc2 in next st) twice, slst in beg ch1 [12]

Rnds 3–4: ch1, sc1 in each st, slst in beg ch1 (2 rnds)

Fasten off.

Add toy safety nose at position shown in diagram, at center front of muzzle, between rnds 1 and 2.

Bottom

Top

Position to attach nose

Tail (make 1)

With Yarn A, make a magic ring.

Rnd 1: ch1 (does not count as a st throughout), sc5 in magic ring, slst in beg ch1 [5]

Place stitch marker in first st of rnd 1 and move it up after each round

Rnd 2: ch1, sc4, sc2 in last st, slst in beg ch1 [6]

Rnds 3–7: ch1, sc1 in each st, slst in beg ch1 (5 rnds)

Fasten off.

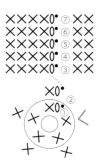

Head (make 1)

With Yarn A, make a magic ring.

Rnd 1: ch1 (does not count as a st throughout), sc6 in magic ring, slst in beg ch1 [6]

Place stitch marker in first st of rnd 1 and move it up after each round

Rnd 2: ch1, (sc2 in next st) 6 times, slst in beg ch1 [12]

Rnd 3: ch1, (sc1, sc2 in next st) 6 times, slst in beg ch1 [18]

Rnd 4: ch1, (sc2, sc2 in next st) 6 times, slst in beg ch1 [24]

Rnds 5–9: ch1, sc1 in each st, slst in beg ch1 (5 rnds)

Rnd 10: ch1, sc8, sc2tog, sc4, sc2tog, sc8, slst in beg ch1 [22]

Rnd 11: ch1, sc4, (sc2tog, sc2) 3 times, sc2tog, sc4, slst in beg ch1 [18]

Rnd 12: ch1, sc1 in each st, slst in beg ch1

Fasten off.

Attach toy safety eyes to front of face at position shown in diagram on page 117, between rnds 8 and 9, leaving 6 sts between eyes.

Center front

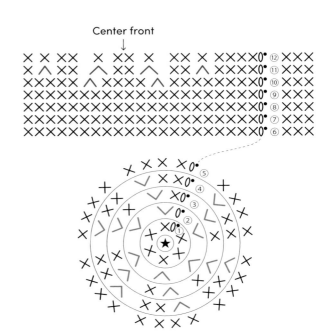

Front Legs (make 2)

With Yarn A, make a magic ring.

Rnd 1: ch1 (does not count as a st throughout), sc7 in magic ring, slst in beg ch1 [7]

Place stitch marker in first st of rnd 1 and move it up after each round

Rnds 2–8: ch1, sc1 in each st, slst in beg ch1 (7 rnds)

Rnd 9: ch1, sc6, sc2 in last st, slst in beg ch1 [8]

Rnd 10: ch1, sc1 in each st, slst in beg ch1

Rnd 11: ch1, sc7, sc2 in last st, slst in beg ch1 [9]

Rnd 12: ch1, sc8, sc2 in last st, slst in beg ch1 [10]

Rnd 13: ch1, sc9, sc2 in lasts st, slst in beg ch1 [11]

Fasten off.

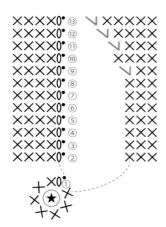

Back Legs (make 2)

With Yarn A, make a magic ring.

Rnd 1: ch1 (does not count as a st throughout), sc7 in magic ring, slst in beg ch1 [7]

Place stitch marker in first st of rnd 1 and move it up after each round

Rnds 2–7: ch1, sc1 in each st, slst in beg ch1 (6 rnds)

Rnd 8: ch1, sc3, sc5 in next st, sc3, slst in beg ch1 [11]

Rnd 9: ch1, sc5, sc5 in next st, sc5, slst in beg ch1 [15]

Rnd 10: ch1, sc7, sc3 in next st, sc7, slst in beg ch1 [17]

Rnds 11–12: ch1, sc1 in each st, slst in beg ch1 (2 rnds)

Rnd 13: ch1, sc6, sc2tog, sc1, sc2tog, sc6, slst in beg ch1 [15]

Fasten off.

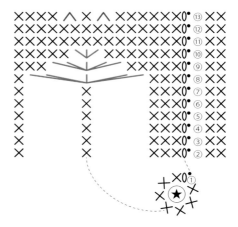

GRAFTING & FINISHING

Location	Yarn Used	Yarn Length
Head	B, C	1¼"–1½" (3–4 cm)
Body	B	1½"–2" (4–5 cm)
Tail	B	3⅛"–3½" (8–9 cm)
Muzzle	B	¾"–1½" (2–4 cm)
Legs	B	1½" (4 cm)
Ears (wrapped ears)	C	4¾" (12 cm)

FINISHED SIZE

8¾" (22 cm) tall × 11¾" (30 cm) long

Grafting the Face

Use this photo as a guide for grafting the fur around the eyes. It may be helpful to mark the placement of the yarn color change using a water-soluble chalk pencil or pins.

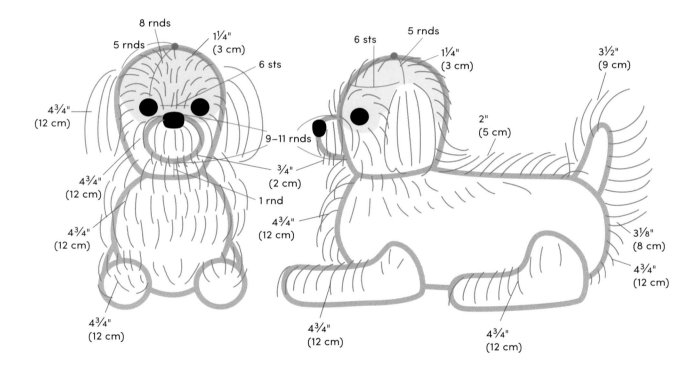

- For grafting, always use a total of 4 strands (2 of the sport weight acrylic and 2 of the light fingering weight acrylic/mohair blend).
- Refer to instructions on page 60 to make the ears with wrapped yarn.
- Graft around the eyes with Yarn C. See photo above for placement.
- Position the eyes and nose on the same level create the classic Shih Tzu expression.
- = Needle felt the areas shaded in light blue in order to compress the yarn and shape the head.

Yorkshire Terrier / Sit

Shown on page 39

TOOLS & MATERIALS

- L/11 (8 mm) crochet hook
- 132 yds (100 g) bulky weight acrylic yarn in light brown
- 27 yds (20 g) bulky weight acrylic yarn in dark gray
- 197 yds (50 g) sport weight acrylic yarn in golden brown
- 79 yds (20 g) of sport weight acrylic yarn in dark gray
- 263 yds (60 g) of light fingering weight acrylic/mohair blend yarn in brown
- 88 yds (20 g) of light fingering weight acrylic/mohair blend yarn in dark gray
- Pair of 15 mm black plastic toy safety eyes
- One 21 mm black plastic toy safety nose
- Polyester fiber fill toy stuffing (about 40 g)
- Stitch marker
- Yarn needle
- Felting needle
- Slicker brush

YARN COMBINATION CHART

Area		Yarn Used		Yarn Color	Strands
Crocheting the Foundation	A	Bulky weight acrylic		Light brown	1 strand
	B	Bulky weight acrylic		Dark gray	1 strand
Grafting the Fur	C	Sport weight acrylic		Golden brown	2 strands
		Light fingering weight acrylic/mohair blend		Brown	2 strands
	D	Sport weight acrylic		Dark gray	2 strands
		Light fingering weight acrylic/mohair blend		Dark gray	1 strand
		Light fingering weight acrylic/mohair blend		Brown	1 strand

CONSTRUCTION STEPS

1. Crochet the body, head, front legs, back legs, ears, muzzle, and tail following instructions on pages 119–121 (also see pages 45–52).

2. Stuff and assemble the body parts following the instructions for the sit pose on pages 53–55.

3. Graft yarn according to the lengths listed on page 122 (refer to pages 56–58 for general grafting instructions).

4. Follow the techniques on page 58 to loosen the yarn and trim the fur into shape. Use the photos at right as a reference.

Front   Side   Back

CROCHET INSTRUCTIONS

Crochet Symbol Key

★ = magic ring

0 = ch st

• = slst

∧ = ⋀ = sc2tog

∨ = ⩔ = sc2 in next st

⩕ = 5 single crochet increase

⬍ = Cluster stitch variation with 3 half double crochet (refer to page 52)

Yarn Color Key

▨ = Yarn A

▨ = Yarn B

Body (make 1)

With Yarn A, make a magic ring.

Rnd 1: ch1 (does not count as a st throughout), sc6 in magic ring, slst in beg ch1 [6]

Place stitch marker in first st of rnd 1 and move it up after each round

Rnd 2: ch1, (sc2 in next st) 6 times, slst in beg ch1 [12]

Rnd 3: ch1, (sc1, sc2 in next st) 6 times, slst in beg ch1 [18]

Rnd 4: ch1, (sc2, sc2 in next st) 6 times, slst in beg ch1 [24]

Rnd 5: ch1, sc2 in next st, sc22, sc2 in next st, change to Yarn B and slst in beg ch1 [26]

Rnds 6–9: in Yarn B ch1, sc5, in Yarn A sc16, in Yarn B sc5, slst in beg ch1 (4 rnds)

Rnd 10: in Yarn B ch1, sc1, sc2tog, sc2, in Yarn A sc16, in Yarn B sc2, sc2tog, sc1, slst in beg ch1 [24]

Rnd 11: in Yarn B ch1, sc4, in Yarn A sc16, in Yarn B sc4, slst in beg ch1

Rnd 12: in Yarn B ch1, sc1, sc2tog, sc2, in Yarn A sc14, in Yarn B sc2, sc2tog, sc1, slst in beg ch1 [22]

Rnd 13: in Yarn B ch1, sc4, in Yarn A sc14, in Yarn B sc4, slst in beg ch1

Rnd 14: in Yarn B ch1, sc1, sc2tog, sc1, in Yarn A (sc4, sc2 in next) twice, sc4, in Yarn B sc1, sc2tog, sc1, slst in beg ch1 [22]

Rnds 15–18: in Yarn B ch1, sc3, in Yarn A sc16, in Yarn B sc3, slst in beg ch1 (4 rnds)

Rnd 19: in Yarn B ch1, sc1, sc2tog, sc1, in Yarn A (sc4, sc2 in next) twice, sc4, in Yarn B sc1, sc2tog, sc1, slst in beg ch1 [22]

Rnds 20–22: in Yarn B ch1, sc3, in Yarn A sc16, in Yarn B sc3, slst in beg ch1 (3 rnds)

Rnd 23: in Yarn B ch1, sc1, sc2tog, in Yarn A sc4, (sc2tog, sc4) twice, in Yarn B sc2tog, sc1, slst in beg ch1 [18]

Fasten off.

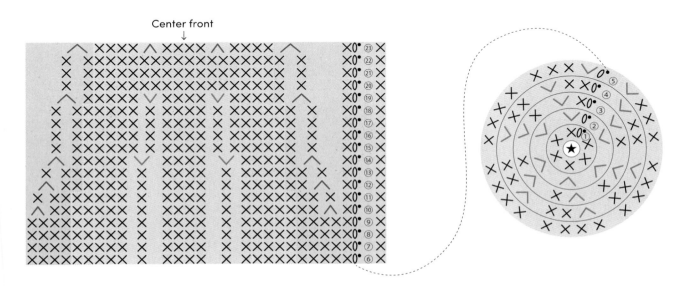

Center front

Head (make 1)

With Yarn A, make a magic ring.

Rnd 1: ch1 (does not count as a st throughout), sc6 in magic ring, slst in beg ch1 [6]

Place stitch marker in first st of rnd 1 and move it up after each round

Rnd 2: ch1, (sc2 in next st) 6 times, slst in beg ch1 [12]

Rnd 3: ch1, (sc1, sc2 in next st) 6 times, slst in beg ch1 [18]

Rnd 4: ch1, (sc2, sc2 in next st) 6 times, slst in beg ch1 [24]

Rnd 5: ch1, (sc3, sc2 in next st) 6 times, slst in beg ch1 [30]

Rnds 6–9: ch1, sc1 in each st, slst in beg ch1 (5 rnds)

Join in Yarn B

Rnd 10: in Yarn B ch1, sc4, in Yarn A sc22, in Yarn B sc4, slst in beg ch1

Rnd 11: in Yarn B, ch1, sc2, sc2tog, in Yarn A sc3, sc2tog, sc2, sc2tog, sc4, sc2tog, sc2, sc2tog, sc3, in Yarn B sc2tog, sc2, slst in beg ch1 [24]

Rnd 12: in Yarn B ch1, sc3, in Yarn A sc5, sc2tog, sc4, sc2tog, sc5, in Yarn B sc3, slst in beg ch1 [22]

Rnd 13: in Yarn B, ch1, sc3, in Yarn A sc1, sc2tog, (sc2, sc2tog) 3 times, sc1, in Yarn B sc3, slst in beg ch1 [18]

Rnd 14: in Yarn B ch1, sc3, in Yarn A sc12, in Yarn A sc3, slst in beg ch1

Fasten off.

Attach toy safety eyes to front of face at position shown in diagram on page 122, between rnds 8 and 9, leaving 6 sts between eyes.

Center front
↓

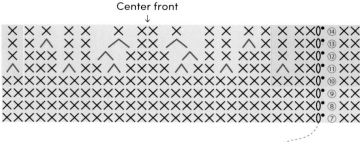

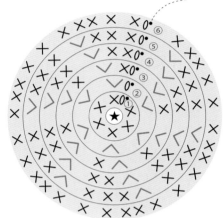

Muzzle (make 1)

With Yarn A, make 5ch.

Rnd 1: skip first ch, sc1 in next ch, sc1 in next 2 ch, sc3 in last ch, rotate and work along opposite side of chain, sc1 in next 2 ch, sc2 in last ch, slst in skipped ch at beg of rnd [10]

Place stitch marker in first st of rnd 1 and move it up after each round

Rnd 2: ch1, (sc4, sc2 in next st) twice, slst in beg ch1 [12]

Rnds 3–4: ch1, sc1 in each st, slst in beg ch1 (2 rnds)

Fasten off.

Add toy safety nose at position shown in diagram, at center front of muzzle, between rnds 1 and 2.

Bottom

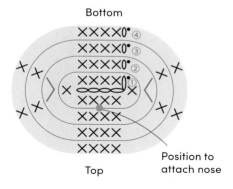

Top

Position to attach nose

Tail (make 1)

With Yarn A, make a magic ring.

Rnd 1: ch1 (does not count as a st throughout), sc5 in magic ring, slst in beg ch1 [5]

Place stitch marker in first st of rnd 1 and move it up after each round

Rnd 2: ch1, sc4, sc2 in last st, slst in beg ch1 [6]

Rnds 3–7: ch1, sc1 in each st, slst in beg ch1 (5 rnds)

Fasten off.

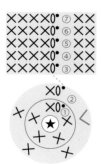

Front Legs (make 2)

With Yarn A, make a magic ring.

Rnd 1: ch1 (does not count as a st throughout), sc8 in magic ring, slst in beg ch1 [8]

Place stitch marker in first st of rnd 1 and move it up after each round

Rnd 2: ch1, sc2, 3hdc-cl in each of next 4 sts, sc2, slst in beg ch1

Rnds 3–8: ch1, sc1 in each st, slst in beg ch1 (6 rnds)

Rnd 9: ch1, sc7, sc2 in next st, slst in beg ch1 [9]

Rnd 10: ch1, sc1 in each st to end, slst in beg ch1

Rnd 11: ch1, sc8, sc2 in next st, slst in beg ch1 [10]

Rnd 12: ch1, sc9, sc2 in next st, slst in beg ch1 [11]

Rnd 13: ch1, sc10, sc2 in next st, slst in beg ch1 [12]

Fasten off.

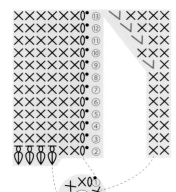

Back Legs (make 2)

With Yarn A, make a magic ring.

Rnd 1: ch1 (does not count as a st throughout), sc8 in magic ring, slst in beg ch1 [8]

Place stitch marker in first st of rnd 1 and move it up after each round

Rnd 2: ch1, sc2, 3hdc-cl in each of next 4 sts, sc2, slst in beg ch1

Rnds 3–8: ch1, sc1 in each st, slst in beg ch1 (6 rnds)

Rnd 9: ch1, sc7, sc2 in next st, slst in beg ch1 [9]

Rnd 10: ch1, sc4, sc5 in next st, sc4, slst in beg ch1 [13]

Rnd 11: ch1, sc6, sc5 in next st, sc6, slst in beg ch1 [17]

Rnds 12–14: ch1, sc1 in each st, slst in beg ch1 (3 rnds)

Rnd 15: ch1, sc5, sc2tog, sc3, sc2tog, sc5, slst in beg ch1 [15]

Fasten off.

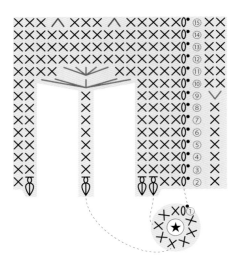

Ears (make 2)

With Yarn A, make a magic ring.

Rnd 1: ch1 (does not count as a st throughout), sc5 in magic ring, slst in beg ch1 [5]

Place stitch marker in first st of rnd 1 and move it up after each round

Rnd 2: ch1, (sc2 in next st) 5 times, slst in beg ch1 [10]

Rnd 3: ch1, sc2 in first st, sc8, sc2 in last st, slst in beg ch1 [12]

Rnd 4: ch1, sc2 in first st, sc10, sc2 in last st, slst in beg ch1 [14]

Rnd 5: ch1, sc2 in first st, sc12, sc2 in last st, slst in beg ch1 [16]

Rnd 6: ch1, sc2 in first st, sc14, sc2 in last st, slst in beg ch1 [18]

Rnd 7: ch1, sc2 in first st, sc16, sc2 in last st, slst in beg ch1 [20]

Fasten off.

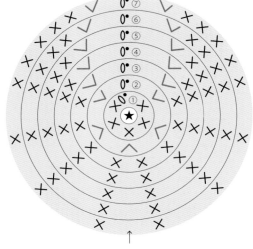

Inner center

9½" (24 cm) tall × 6¾" (17 cm) long

Location	Yarn Used	Yarn Length
Head	C, D	¾"–8" (2–20 cm)
Body	C, D	2"–2½" (5–6 cm)
Tail	C, D	3⅛" (8 cm)
Muzzle	C	4¾" (12 cm)
Legs	C	1¼"–3" (3–5 cm)
Ears	C	1½" (4 cm)

How to Style the Hair

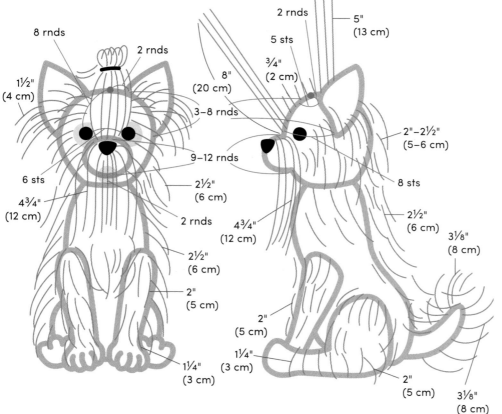

Graft shorter pieces of yarn closest to the top of the head and longer pieces to the forehead.

Arrange the grafted yarn in a bundle.

Use a piece of the same color yarn to tie the bundle together on top of the head.

Fold the bundle and tie it in place, creating a small bun on top of the head. Let the yarn ends flow toward the back of the head.

- For grafting, always use a total of 4 strands (2 of the sport weight acrylic and 2 of the light fingering weight acrylic/mohair blend).
- Graft from the back of the head to the tail with Yarn D.
- Style the hair and attach a ribbon to finish as shown in the photos at right
- Brush the front and back with a slicker brush before grafting the ears. Graft the fur to the lower portions of the ears.
- Do not graft fur to the paws.
- ▢ = Needle felt the areas shaded in light blue in order to compress the yarn and shape the eyes and chin.

Bichon Frise / Stand

Shown on page 41

TOOLS & MATERIALS

- P/15 (10 mm) crochet hook
- 655 yds (470 g) bulky weight acrylic yarn in white
- Pair of 15 mm black plastic toy safety eyes
- One 21 mm black plastic toy safety nose
- Polyester fiber fill toy stuffing (about 120 g)
- Stitch marker
- Yarn needle
- Felting needle
- Slicker brush

YARN COMBINATION CHART

Area	Yarn Used		Yarn Color	Amount	Strands
Crocheting the Foundation	A	Acrylic bulky weight	White	357 yds (270 g)	2 strands
Grafting the Fur	B	Acrylic bulky weight	White	298 yds (200 g)	2 strands

CONSTRUCTION STEPS

1. Crochet the body, head, front legs, back legs, ears, muzzle, and tail following instructions on pages 124–126 (also see pages 45–52).

2. Stuff and assemble the body parts following the instructions for the stand pose on pages 54–55.

3. Graft yarn according to the lengths listed on page 127 (refer to pages 56–58 for general grafting instructions).

4. Follow the techniques on page 58 to loosen the yarn and trim the fur into shape. Use the photos below as a reference.

Front   Side   Back

CROCHET INSTRUCTIONS

Crochet Symbol Key

★ = magic ring   ∧ = ⋀ = sc2tog

0 = ch st   ∨ = ⋎ = sc2 in next st

• = slst

Body (make 1)

With Yarn A, make a magic ring.

Rnd 1: ch1 (does not count as a st throughout), sc6 in magic ring, slst in beg ch1 [6]

Place stitch marker in first st of rnd 1 and move it up after each round.

Rnd 2: ch1, (sc2 in next st) 6 times, slst in beg ch1 [12]

Rnd 3: ch1, (sc1, sc2 in next st) 6 times, slst in beg ch1 [18]

Rnd 4: ch1, (sc2, sc2 in next st) 6 times, slst in beg ch1 [24]

Rnd 5: ch1, (sc3, sc2 in next st) 6 times, slst in beg ch1 [30]

Rnds 6–24: ch1, sc1 in each st, slst in beg ch1 (19 rnds)

Rnd 25: ch1, (sc3, sc2tog) 6 times, slst in beg ch1 [24]

Rnd 26: ch1, (sc2, sc2tog) 6 times, slst in beg ch1 [18]

Begin to stuff body firmly.

Rnd 27: ch1, (sc1, sc2tog) 6 times, slst in beg ch1 [12]

Rnd 28: ch1, (sc2tog) 6 times, slst in beg ch1 [6]

Fasten off leaving a long tail end. Add more stuffing if needed then thread yarn through stitches of last round and pull tightly to close.

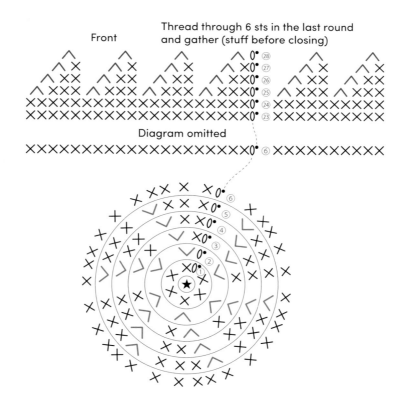

Front

Thread through 6 sts in the last round and gather (stuff before closing)

Diagram omitted

Head (make 1)

With Yarn A, make a magic ring.

Rnd 1: ch1 (does not count as a st throughout), sc6 in magic ring, slst in beg ch1 [6]

Place stitch marker in first st of rnd 1 and move it up after each round

Rnd 2: ch1, (sc2 in next st) 6 times, slst in beg ch1 [12]

Rnd 3: ch1, (sc1, sc2 in next st) 6 times, slst in beg ch1 [18]

Rnd 4: ch1, (sc2, sc2 in next st) 6 times, slst in beg ch1 [24]

Rnd 5: ch1, (sc3, sc2 in next st) 6 times, slst in beg ch1 [30]

Rnds 6–10: ch1, sc1 in each st, slst in beg ch1 (5 rnds)

Rnd 11: ch1, sc2, sc2tog, sc3, sc2tog, sc2, sc2tog, sc4, sc2tog, sc2, sc2tog, sc3, sc2tog, sc2, slst in beg ch1 [24]

Rnd 12: ch1, sc8, sc2tog, sc4, sc2tog, sc8, slst in beg ch1 [22]

Rnd 13: ch1, sc4, (sc2tog, sc2) 3 times, sc2tog, sc4, slst in beg ch1 [18]

Rnd 14: ch1, sc1 in each st, slst in beg ch1

Fasten off.

Attach toy safety eyes to front of face at position shown in diagram on page 127, between rnds 8 and 9, leaving 6 sts between eyes.

Center front

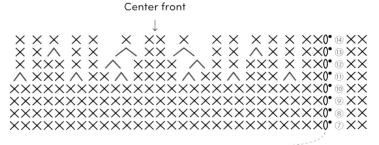

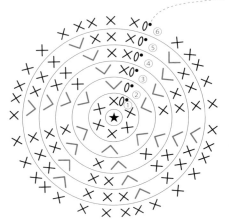

Front Legs (make 2)

With Yarn A, make a magic ring.

Rnd 1: ch1 (does not count as a st throughout), sc5 in magic ring, slst in beg ch1 [5]

Place stitch marker in first st of rnd 1 and move it up after each round

Rnd 2: ch1, (sc2 in next st) 5 times, slst in beg ch1 [10]

Rnds 3–11: ch1, sc1 in each st, slst in beg ch1 (9 rnds)

Fasten off.

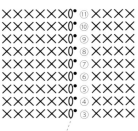

Back Legs (make 2)

With Yarn A, make a magic ring.

Rnd 1: ch1 (does not count as a st throughout), sc5 in magic ring, slst in beg ch1 [5]

Place stitch marker in first st of rnd 1 and move it up after each round

Rnd 2: ch1, (sc2 in next st) 5 times, slst in beg ch1 [10]

Rnds 3–10: ch1, sc1 in each st, slst in beg ch1 (8 rnds)

Fasten off.

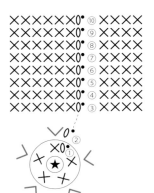

Ears (make 2)

With Yarn A, make 4ch, leaving a 12" (30 cm) tail of yarn.
Work in rows.
Row 1: sc1 in second ch from hook, sc1 in each remaining ch, turn [3]
Row 2: ch1 (does not count as a st throughout), sc2 in first st, sc1, sc2 in last st, turn [5]
Rows 3–4: ch1, sc1 in each st to end, turn
Fasten off.

Bottom

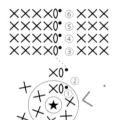

Leave a 12" (30 cm)
yarn tail

Top

Muzzle (make 1)

With Yarn A, make 5ch.
Rnd 1: skip first ch, sc1 in next ch, sc1 in next 2 ch, sc3 in last ch, rotate and work along opposite side of chain, sc1 in next 2 ch, sc2 in last ch, slst in skipped ch at beg of rnd [10]
Place stitch marker in first st of rnd 1 and move it up after each round.
Rnd 2: ch1, (sc4, sc2 in next st) twice, slst in beg ch1 [12]
Rnds 3–4: ch1, sc1 in each st to end, slst in beg ch1 (2 rnds)
Fasten off.
Add toy safety nose at position shown in diagram, at center front of muzzle, between rnds 1 and 2.

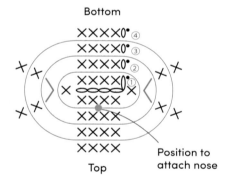

Bottom

Position to
attach nose

Top

Tail (make 1)

With Yarn A, make a magic ring.
Rnd 1: ch1 (does not count as a st throughout), sc6 in magic ring, slst in beg ch1 [6]
Place stitch marker in first st of rnd 1 and move it up after each round
Rnd 2: ch1, sc5, sc2 in next st, slst in beg ch1 [7]
Rnds 3–6: ch1, sc1 in each st, slst in beg ch1 (4 rnds)
Fasten off.

FINISHED SIZE

13" (33 cm) tall × 13" (33 cm) long

Location	Yarn Used	Yarn Length
Head	B	1¼"–1½" (3–4 cm)
Body		¾"–1½" (2–4 cm)
Tail		1½" (4 cm)
Muzzle		¾" (2 cm)
Legs		3
Ears		2–2.5

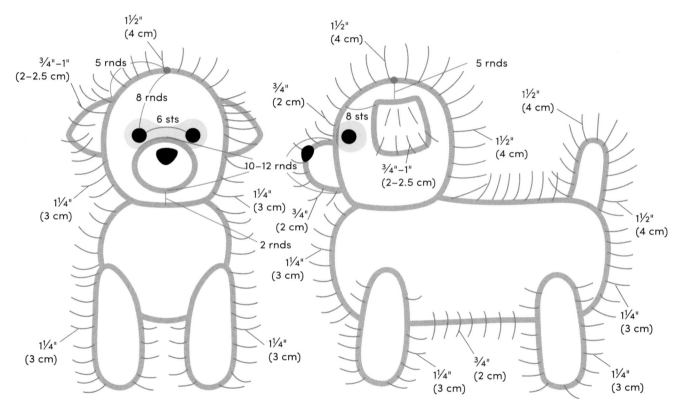

- For grafting, use two strands of acrylic bulky weight yarn.
- When grafting yarn to the ears, keep the round the silhouette of the head in mind.
-    = Needle felt the areas shaded in light blue in order to compress the yarn and shape the eyes.
- Do not graft yarn on the paws because it will make it difficult for the dog to stand.
- Continue trimming and brushing the fur until you achieve the desired shape.

Basic Crochet Symbols & Stitches

Chain stitch: Wrap the yarn around the hook (yarn over) and pull the yarn through the loop on the hook.

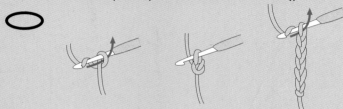

Slip stitch: Insert the hook into the stitch as instructed, yarn over, pull the yarn back through the stitch and also through the loop on the hook.

Single crochet: To work back along a line of chain stitches, skip the first chain stitch, insert the hook into the top half of the next chain stitch (the second chain stitch from the hook), yarn over, pull the yarn through the chain stitch (two loops are now on the hook), yarn over and pull through both loops.

First chain stitch | When working into a row or round of single crochet stitches, you will start the row or round with a chain 1 (this does not usually count as a stitch), then you will work 1 single crochet into each stitch, always placing the hook under both loops at the top of the single crochet stitch.

2 single crochet in the next stitch: Make two single crochet in the same stitch.

2 stitches   Increase 1 stitch

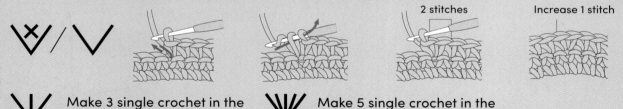

Make 3 single crochet in the same stitch   Make 5 single crochet in the same stitch

Single crochet 2 together: Decrease 1 stitch by working 2 stitches together as follows: Insert hook into next stitch, yarn over and pull loop through, insert hook into next stitch, yarn over and pull a loop through (3 loops on hook), yarn over and pull through all 3 loops.

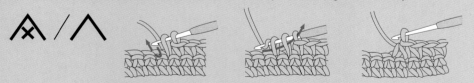

Single crochet 3 together: Decrease 2 stitches by working 3 stitches together as follows: *Insert hook into next stitch, yarn over and pull loop through* repeat from * to * in next 2 stitches (4 loops on hook), yarn over and pull through all 4 loops.